SELECTIONS FROM
SPEECHES
(1900–1959)

SELECTIONS

FROM

SPEECHES

(1900–1959)

OF

MURRAY SEASONGOOD

Compiled WITH *Foreword* AND *Head Notes* BY

AGNES SEASONGOOD

Alfred·A·Knopf　NEW YORK

1960

L. C. catalog card number: 60–10498

© AGNES SEASONGOOD, 1960

THIS IS A BORZOI BOOK,
PUBLISHED BY ALFRED A. KNOPF, INC.

FIRST EDITION

Foreword

THE LATE Martha S. Stern, of Cincinnati, a sister of my husband, created a trust that commissioned me to compile and publish a book containing selections from speeches made by him and which would reflect her brother's interests and services. This volume is intended to carry out her wishes.

Murray Seasongood was born in Cincinnati, October 27, 1878, and, except for absences during his education, has lived there ever since. He attended the public schools of Cincinnati and Edgeborough, a school in Guildford, England. He received his A.B. from Harvard in 1900, his M.A. in 1901, and his LL.B. in 1903. In college he was elected an honorary member of Phi Beta Kappa and, at the law school, life secretary of his class. While at Harvard he had his first experience in teaching, conducting classes in English composition at the Prospect Union in Cambridgeport. He also had a wide experience in writing, speaking, and debating. Thus, in this last, he was frequently presiding or other officer, participant, adviser, judge or coach, president of the Harvard Debating Union, and member of various debating teams, one of which was the Harvard Varsity team that debated Yale. He also had a role in selecting the Wellesley team in the great struggle against Vassar, the first women's intercollegiate debate. All of this helped fit him ". . . to speak in public on the stage" in later years.

Following his admission to the Ohio Bar in 1903, his principal occupation has been as a lawyer. However, the variety of his other activities has been great: speaker, writer, teacher, student, consultant, politician, reformer, and participant in numerous public, semi-public, philanthropic, and cultural affairs. The editor of *The Practical Lawyer* (published by The American Law Institute) in a foreword to a 1956 article by my husband, "What Employments Must a Lawyer Accept?" had this to say:

> *Murray Seasongood is a member of the Ohio Bar but his many public services and educational ventures support a presumption that here is not one man but two or more sharing the same name.*

In connection with his varied activities, he has made any number of talks. They have been in most of the states of the Union, the District of Columbia, and in places so far apart as Portland, Maine; San Antonio, Texas; Tuscaloosa, Alabama; Niagara Falls, Canada; San Juan, Puerto Rico; Honolulu, Hawaii; and London. A considerable number of the talks selected relate to government and law, judges, lawyers, and legal procedures. However, his talks have been over a wide range of subjects, on many different occasions and before many different kinds of audiences. He has spoken at religious congregations, men's and women's colleges, schools, convocations, political, luncheon, Masonic, and other clubs and gatherings, often as presiding officer, toastmaster, or master of ceremonies. He was particularly pleased to have served in such capacities at both his college and law-school class's fiftieth reunion banquets in June 1950 and in June 1953 at the Boston Harvard Club.

It has been hard to choose these few selections from his many talks. Some of those included will, I hope, make apparent my husband's firm conviction that local government is the most important of the three levels of government, and that knowledge of it and of the law relating to it, coupled with active and enthusiastic participation on an unselfish basis, especially by young people, is essential for the well-being of our country. The comments under some of the headings of the speeches, or the extracts, are meant to have a bearing not only on the subject matter, but, as well, on the speaker's life, character, and efforts.

The difficulty of selection was intensified because my husband has rarely written out addresses in advance except where he knew his remarks would be wanted for publication. Almost always he spoke without notes or with a few key words or a scanty outline on cards, and, as comparatively few of his talks were taken in shorthand and transcribed, some of those I should like to have had in the book could not be reconstructed or included. For example: as an address indicative of his interest in the blind, his response when, on April 16, 1959, he was made an honorary life member of the Cincinnati Association for the Blind, of which he had been for many years before a member of the Executive Committee; or his address at the fiftieth anniversary of Clovernook Home and School for the Blind on May 8, 1953, an institution conducted by the Trader sisters, his classmates and lifelong friends. My husband acted for years as counsel for the Home, which grew and prospered.

Recently, when it was incorporated, he became one of its five trustees. More than fifty years ago his work for the blind began by weekly reading to groups at the public library from the plays of Shakespeare, their chosen author. For a number of years he has served, too, as vice-president of the Cincinnati Library Society for the Blind. About 1912 he was appointed by Governor White a member of the Ohio Commission for the Blind and reappointed by successive governors until, on entering public life, he resigned. And he has been useful to the blind in many other respects.

I should like, also, to have illustrated his interest in people of the Negro race by including one of his many addresses to them, such as at one of the earliest celebrations of his election as Mayor, in Calvary Methodist Church, or his address "Father Oxley as a Harvard Man," at the testimonial program and reception in St. Andrew's Episcopal Church for the Reverend E. H. Oxley, in recognition of that wonderful Cincinnati Negro preacher's forty years of service there. My husband was instrumental in having the first person of Negro race, a woman, now a distinguished doctor, admitted to the Cincinnati Medical School, and also the first Negro pupil in what was known as the Y.M.C.A. Night Law School.

As helping to show the diversity of causes my husband espoused and on which he expressed himself forcibly, I mention his unsuccessful appeal to the Cincinnati School Board to abolish fraternities and sororities in the public high schools as illegal and injurious to the democratic spirit that should prevail there. But no record is available of his addresses to the board, or of his remarks in the course of public debate over the radio, or of the address he delivered on the subject to the Western Hills Masonic Club.

In an attempt to keep the book within reasonable limits, I have frequently, without showing where omissions occur, printed only brief extracts from the full speech or have made cuts, some perhaps too drastic.

In all instances where the speeches have previously appeared in other publications, permission to reprint portions of them has been graciously granted.

AGNES SEASONGOOD

Cincinnati, *November* 1959

Contents

xii

CONTENTS

SELECTIONS FROM
SPEECHES
(1900–1959)

⇒⇒-⇒⇒-⇒⇒-⇒⇒-⇒⇒-⇒⇒≪≪-≪≪-≪≪-≪≪-≪≪-≪≪

Ivy Oration

(JUNE 1900)

*Elected Ivy orator by the class of 1900, Murray Sea-
songood delivered this speech on Class Day in
Sanders Theatre. It is printed in full in* The Harvard
Advocate, *Vol. 49, No. 10 (June 27, 1900). For
other glimpses of Harvard and Harvard personages
of the period, see his "Cambridge Re-Visited," in*
Social Science, *Vol. 25, No. 4 (Oct. 1950), p. 223,
and "Harvard Worthies of the 1890's," in* Social
Science, *Vol. 20, No. 3 (July 1945), p. 129.*

YOU ARE probably curious to know by what license I
speak, in this town that allows none. People have always
wondered why this particular—or rather very general—
talk should be, even after the Ivy orator has explained.
Let me preserve the tradition.

The class of once upon a time—which is another way
of saying sixty-five—decided for some reason to plant ivy.
Accordingly the class invited one of its more serious members (there were serious members even before the *Harvard Monthly*) to bid the sprig come out and try, or
rather, try and come out. Stenographic reports say his
speech ended thus: "Even as this plant, so may the influence of our class grow and spread." When orators had
spoken several years, and always to the discouragement
of the ivy, classes came to console themselves by saying

3

bad things of the speaker, and he retorted with bad jokes on the class. They exchange pleasantries to this day. I represent the exchange.

The truth is that the world has improved, the past 2,500 years, in all things save its jokes. So Ivy orators have had to try various devices with varying success. One of the more timorous, to soften his hearers, began by saying farewell. Mr. John Jay Chapman started his "Practical Agitations" with a defense of the faculty. At least three of my predecessors must have failed to say all they wanted, because now as professors here they talk every day for an hour, yes, and over the hour! Other favorite subterfuges were to complain of Memorial board,[1] of U. 4, of the college choir, or to insist that one's class was not the most brilliant ever graduated. But I can do none of these! Surely Memorial food is beyond reproach now. I have never found U. 4 [2] humorous, though I have seen people smile there. Nor does the college choir bother me: I can't hear it from my room. And I insist that 1900, far from being commonplace, is the first class of the century—that is, the twentieth!

So I was constrained to try a new plan. "Let's change places," I said to the poet. But he replied: "I fear me, no! Poets are not made, they are born. I was born, some fifteen years ago; it is, therefore, *chose jugée.*"

Since this rebuff, I have led "the strenuous life." Whenever a thing struck me as funny, I tried it on my friends, shaking with laughter myself to encourage them. They invariably pronounced it extravagant or cheap, or if they came from Boston, claimed it as an heirloom,

[1] Memorial Hall was the large common eating place.
[2] The office of Dean Briggs.

4

handed down four generations in their family. In despair
I burrowed through old funny papers like the "Crimes-
done" (Crimson) in its reviews and editorial sallies, but
the same old jests were constantly reappearing there. The
longer I waited, the less all things seemed a joke! Then I
recalled suddenly what Tusitala, great chief of the Samo-
ans—whose English name is Stevenson—once said, that
"Art consists in leaving out things." Clearly, then, the art
of an Ivy orator is leaving out the jokes! At all events
each, as compared to his predecessor, must be a succeeding speaker.

Such logic is one of the gains from four years of study!
Let me recall more, let me tell—oh, classmates—the story
of our lives! (Will the music above please to play trem-
ulously?) Ah, but we were a sad and sorry lot that first
October with great mocking green registration cards! One
man, I know, asked his adviser what time the next train
left for far, far away Mauch Chunk and was grieved to
find him not omniscient. (Note: this adviser was not of
the English Department.) But there is nothing like a
Rush for bringing men into contact, and we bumped fear-
lessly, not stopping even to dress our naked wounds. As
soon as we had recovered from the punches, we bought
sketchbooks for our courses: learned in fine arts that
Dagon was not god of Dagos, but that of tropical Egypt,
Isis; in history, heard of the "terrible Turk," and that
Attila couldn't invade Germany because of the Oder:
even German Cologne didn't help him.

Well, plus one summer and a pipe, and minus the
first year's docility, we were sophomores, each realizing
for the first time what a splendid fellow he was! Then
did we call vague things vaguer names, which is psychol-

5

ogy, and read also philosophy, or the disproving what the man before you said.

Junior year found us searching for the special issue—especially of banks. We had come by now to know the Widow's might;[3] had resolved ourselves semiannually into cyclopedias, of which our bluebooks were sadly abridged editions; had been up on Shakespeare before, and down on him after the troublous times. Incidentally we went into athletics so hard that even the cricket team showed tremendous in crease.

Last fall we were confronted with ethical questions such as: do you drink? do you sing? are you married? These were asked by the cruel secretary, eager to have our lives. The answers are to furnish Sunday School tracts. Accordingly we spent half the year deciding to write them, another half in the writing, and the odd moments remaining, in having our pictures taken. This last caused some men who had not done so before to acquire the habit of looking pleasant. But the great deed for which 1900 will always be remembered is its electing the special committee that danced the class last night into a wilted collar and a dejected shirt.

Still, when all is said, which will be in some hours now, to whom do we owe most—always after the Bursar (as he seems always after us)? "Great wits," says the Dean, Swift, "love to strike at the highest objects." I shall now briefly demolish the faculty. But, like Homer, or his follower who just spoke, had I a hundred tongues (and you will begin to think soon that I have), I could not tell of all their wondrous deeds. Knowing the fondness of Cambridge people for coming early to lectures, their latest

[3] Cramming by a local coach known as the Widow.

venture, strangely enough, is introducing eight o'clocks to get us up, and a three years' course to get us out. Great bodies move slowly. Aware, after two centuries and a half, of how far the dormitories were from godliness, our faculty (for mistakes) put in showers and raised each man's rent $37,000. One of the English Department [4] discovered recently double-edged daggers in the catalogue, and as many stars as all the astronomers. He feared the fatuous infatuation of young instructors, and much else, O Radcliffe of thee! that thou wouldst make of sweet girl graduates Bachelors, aye and worse, Masters of Harvard!

Returning from the Washington Elm—oh, History 10, spare that tree—to U. 5 (the faculty room). This summer they are to welcome Cuban teachers, to whom we have bequeathed our bedding and blessing, but who, we trust, will not "take up our beds and walk." [5] Next season it is to be Puerto Ricans, and the year after, Filipinos, headed by Aggie himself, to help the Mott Haven in the sprints, and his importers by giving military science!

Now let us move to Helicon—or Orrington, "lest we forget" the Maine man (the poet) and his little ditty. In a few days, classmates, after four years of practice in the gym, we are to be put through our final exercises in this theater, to be turned out with the Harvard finish, or Commencement—though according to the French, *venir* is

[4] This was Professor Barrett Wendell. The extent to which these fears have eventuated since then and how far they have been justified by time is amusingly detailed in an article appearing in the *Harvard Alumni Bulletin* (Oct. 10, 1959), p. 69, quoting President Conant's famous "Harvard is not co-educational in theory, only in practice."

[5] This was suggested by the speaker's friend, the late Charles T. Copeland, famous as "Copey."

"to come." We are to leave our *alma mater* for our parents proper, or else tread alone the big, rough world outside the Yard. It is, I have often felt, a Noah's-ark-like Yard (I do not refer now to the winter floods) with its little square and stiff red houses, its little sorrows and—little time for talk. I must not transgress more on the poet's "sweet complaining grievance."

We separate soon to do divers things. Some to argue before the courts—if ever they get a chance—so a man assaulted may perhaps recover; or if he cannot, contest his will for the deed. Sixty-six of us will become saturated with learning till we drip knowledge or issue books hidebound. Some of our number will pursue metaphysical or other speculations, till their wealth is all in coppers. Some, I fear, will be loyal to a trust; others, like modern St. Georges, puncture the dragon octopuses. Some few will help chase Aguinaldo—that business promises permanence—as "men behind the guns"; and not a few will take good care never to get in front of them, preferring to lay out new dependencies, rather than dependants.

But whatever we do, let us remember that little should be harder to endure than the Ivy oration! Also, that if opportunity makes the man, so does he often make the opportunity; and after all, life must be pleasant: so many people have complained that it is short.

>>>->>>->>>->>>->>>->>)(((-(((-(((-(((-(((-(((

Commencement Past and Present

(JUNE 1900)

*Chosen by a committee of the faculty, Murray Sea-
songood gave the following commencer's part or
"dissertation" at Harvard commencement in Sanders
Theatre. It is reprinted from* The Harvard Advocate
*(of which he was an editor), Vol. 49, No. 10
(June 27, 1900). For additional Harvard history, his
"Our Campo Santo" (the burial place, across from
the Yard, of Harvard's first president, Henry Dun-
ster, and of other early Harvard presidents) in* The
Harvard Advocate, *Class Day Number 1899, will
be of interest.*

In 1642, when Harvard graduated her first class, nine
bachelors, "the Governor, the Magistrates and Ministers
from all parts, with all sorts of Scholars, were present,
and did hear their exercises." Then, having dined together in Commons, they sang a psalm and were well
content.

What made those first commencements possible, despite poverty and danger, is evident from a note like
this: "Just as morn exercise ended, Mr. Cotton Mather's
child dies, yet he preaches at Charlestown in the afternoon." Such purpose and power to endure, engendered
freedom of thought and the strength to speak one's belief.

The chief part of the exercises, from the earliest times
down to the Revolution, consisted of theses assigned to

9

the best scholars, who maintained them syllogistically in Latin against the class. A glance shows Harvard to have been then, as now, liberal.

Thus in problems of philosophy, at a time when Oxford scholars read Aristotle on their knees, and at graduation swore to defend his philosophy, Harvard commencers confined themselves to no one system, but chose from each what they believed right. So too in science—or what passed for science—commencement speakers here readily admitted the circulation of the blood, and the efficacy of vaccination.

Large-mindedness showed itself even in religious disputation. Harvard was founded as a school of divinity. Yet at its first commencement not one of the fifty-seven questions discussed had to do with matters of faith. "Later," says the Magnalia, "the Masters presumed to fly as high as divinity of the reformed stamp." We smile at serious argument purporting to show that "Samson did not commit suicide in the temple of the Philistines" or that "When Baalam's ass spoke there was no change in its organs"; but in such an age, from the midst of a narrow Puritanism, what a doctrine is this: "The toleration of every religion promotes true religion."

The best proof of the catholicity of these disputes is the offense they gave. Judge Dudley, in 1730, rose and entered his public protest against a dispute regarding the eternity of Christ. A minister of the Gospel from Boston, shocked, another time, by a denial of the perfection of God's knowledge, turned his back, left the house, and penned to the president a long protest "against young men sharpening their Wits on their Maker." President Holyoke replied that he was pleased to see one so jealous for the Divine Honor, but could not believe young men less religious than they had been in his correspondent's day. The difference in breadth of view between his reply and the minister's pompous mixture of Biblical quotation and paraphrased proverb is astonishing indeed.

What makes commencements of this first period chiefly a source of pride, however, is their patriotism. In 1743 Samuel Adams declared: "It is lawful to resist the Chief Magistrate, if the state cannot otherwise be preserved!" One can see in such a doctrine, spoken before governor and crown officers, beginnings of a revolution! And a further step in Elbridge Gerry's contention, the year of the Stamp Act, that "the new prohibitory duties, which made it useless for the people to engage in commerce, may be evaded by them as faithful subjects." The class of a year or so later appeared by special vote to take its degrees in untaxed, home-manufactured garments. Small wonder commencement was not celebrated during the Revolution: Harvard men were supporting their convictions in arms!

All in all, then, colonial commencements show the college to have been abreast in science, religion, and politics, with the best thought of the country. And the parts must have had some effect, for they were spoken on New England's great holiday. We are accustomed to think of the Puritan as always in the pulpit; but on commencement he came down! The governing bodies had indulged in occasional discussions too—not always of a serious nature —whether, for instance, to have plum cake (which may be served, you will recall, with hard or brandy sauce) is dishonorable to the college. Several times they decided it is, and then weakly recanted.

But it was immediately after the Revolution that commencement entered its halcyon period, which lasted almost to the middle of our century. Poor and rich alike
enjoyed the day. Booths covered the Common; business
was suspended for leagues about; the graduates of the
year, dressed in many colored magnificence, entertained
becomingly all the fashion of Boston.

In the exercises English, which had insinuated itself
somehow, and contemporary thought and events began
to crowd on Greek, Latin, and the Bible. Holmes read an
English poem. In the thirties a candidate for the M.A.
spoke on transcendentalism, which the Reverend John
Pierce "supposed captivating to a few irregular geniuses,
but which to him was like the tale of an idiot, full of
sound and fury, signifying nothing." Men someday to be
great orators, among them John Quincy Adams, Everett,
and Phillips, spoke English orations. A mention, in the
year of Waterloo, of the deposed imperial despot of
France gained loud applause. So did Valedictorian Josiah
Quincy's words on Lafayette, when the great man was
present to receive an honorary degree.

A commencement of this or of the preceding period
combined with the dignity of the present ceremonies a
charm now confined to Class Day. (As early as 1674,
when Judge Sewall took his degree, "his future wife was
present, and set her affections on him, as he learned after
their marriage.") For there had been no Class Day to
speak of; indeed, it was a day unspeakable until President
Quincy, aiming at greater decorum, diverted the "young-
lady" element to the newer festival by means of music
and dancing.

This was a severe blow to commencement, from which

it has never recovered. No one, I think, regrets stripping the day of its former excessive pomp. There is enough dignity in the modern commencement, and a constantly increasing size to the procession of loyal graduates that sweeps round the Yard. But for the senior, commencement has lost much of its glory. National holidays and the increase of institutions of learning which share New England's loyalty lessen its former local significance. Within the college the freedom that accompanies the elective system has made an end of compulsory parts on assigned subjects. Wider undergraduate activities, too— thesis and research work for courses, prizes and scholarships, and, during the past generation, undergraduate publications, the general tendency toward writing rather than speaking—all combine to deprive commencers' parts of the important place once theirs.

Just how future commencements will be celebrated is at present uncertain. A common undergraduate opinion is that the splendor of Class Day makes anything that comes after it an anticlimax; that commencers' parts are now superfluous; and that the day should be surrendered entirely to the graduate. Opposed to this view are those who look on commencers' parts as a tradition with two centuries and a half behind it, and bid us spare the traditions we have. There is still, they insist, lively outside interest in the parts. Then, too, they permit a man to say what he has thought about. Surely, in preserving them, seniors can be made to feel they have an important duty!

Which of these opinions prevails, and in what manner the country's oldest festival, Thanksgiving aside, is to be continued, succeeding classes must largely determine.

-»»-»»-»»-»»-»»-»»«««-«««-«««-«««-«««-«««

Some Law in Shakespeare

(APRIL 21, 1908)

This address was given before the Cincinnati Bar Association, and is reprinted, with omission of supporting authorities used, from the Ohio Law Reporter, Vol. 6, p. 327. Murray Seasongood became a president of the association and, over a long period, chairman or member of various committees, including the Joint Committee of the Association and the Lawyers Club on Selection of Judges. He was also representative of the association in the House of Delegates, American Bar Association.

IN THIS PAPER I do not attempt to discuss or decide whether Shakespeare was ever a lawyer's clerk, as contended by Malone, J. Payne Collier, and other Shakespeareans, or whether, as the late Cushman K. Davis and others have thought, he derived his knowledge of law merely from study of it. Neither shall I try to settle the much mooted question of whether Shakespeare was Bacon. Nor am I greatly concerned with showing Shakespeare's law impeccable. That the use of law terms by "pleasant Will" is, however, extraordinarily accurate is generally conceded. He uses the jargon of the law, the words of art, with technical knowledge and precision. Lord Bramwell wrote a treatise on the law of *Shylock v. Antonio*. So careful an author as Best on Evidence has cited *Othello* (III, 3) to show that what a man (Cassio) says while asleep is not evidence against him. Professor Beale quotes as correct law in an article in the January 1908 *Harvard Law Review* on Contempt of Court, L. C. J. Gascoigne's committal of Henry V, then Prince of Wales, for striking him as recounted in *Henry IV*, part 2 (v, 2):

> "I, then did use the person of your father;
> The image of his power lay then in me . . .
> whereon, as an offender to your father, I give
> bold way to my authority, And did commit
> you."

So, too, our Ohio Supreme Court has recently held violation of an injunction an offense against justice, and as punishable by a court other than that which issued the order.

Shakespeare's will, wherein he leaves to his wife nothing but his second best bed, has been regarded by the charitable as only another indication of the decedent's legal knowledge that his wife would be entitled to dower in his real estate, of which he had considerable. On the other hand, it has been argued that the will was drawn by one ignorant of law and was void, for pretermitting therein a child of the testator. Mr. Charles Allen in "Notes on the Bacon-Shakespeare Question" has propounded the dilemma that the bond in the *Merchant of Venice* was either void as against public policy and therefore utterly unenforceable; or, if not, then Portia's law, allowing the pound of flesh but no drop of blood, violated the maxim that everything necessary to the enjoyment of a grant goes with it. Or, as another writer has put it, the heart cannot be hypothecated so as to furnish ground for a suit, except in a court of love.

The object of this paper is to explain some otherwise confusing passages, and to hang on them as a peg a lantern (which will, I am afraid, smoke somewhat) showing what a crude and harsh science the law was as Shakespeare knew it, and so to make you more tolerant of its present shortcomings—if the perfection of reason still have any!

See how rigidly it was applied: *Quo warranto* is designed, *inter alia*, to oust from an office one who fills it without authority. Thomas à Becket, after being murdered, was sued in such an action and required to show cause why he should not be ousted from the office of Saint, which it was alleged he was usurping. Four centuries after his interment he was cited at the instance of Henry VIII to appear before the Star Chamber and answer for his crimes: he was sentenced, and his bones were burned and scattered to the winds.

Gratiano says to Shylock:

> *Thy currish spirit Govern'd a wolf, who, hanged*
> *   for human slaughter,*
> *Even from the gallows did his fell soul fleet,* . . .
> *Infused itself in thee; for thy desires Are wolfish,*
> *   bloody, starved and ravenous."*

You will not be surprised to learn, then, that Shakespeare was familiar with the practice, prevailing chiefly on the continent, of trying criminally, sentencing, and executing animals for their crimes. A wolf was so hanged in Ansbach in 1685. Cotton Mather in his *Magnalia* tells how at New Haven, Connecticut, in 1662, a cow was executed at the gallows. Today, in Montenegro, animals are tried and convicted for homicide, and a *"Schweinfurter Sauhenker"* is a term of opprobrium to designate a low fellow, because the executioner of Schweinfurt in 1576 hanged a pig without legal authority.

Recall, if you please, also, the trial in Racine's *Les Plaideurs* in which a dog is condemned to the galleys for stealing a capon, but respited through euphoniously, if inexactly, the tears of its puppies.

Animals not domestic, which could not be brought into court by seizure, were sentenced after formal publication of summons from the pulpit and trial by anathema. Thus arose the custom, in persons not clerkly, and so not privileged to curse offenders, of exhorting in rhyme, or otherwise, troublesome animals which could not be caught, to leave. The thunders of Ernulphus echo faintly in Orlando's verses to Rosalind:

I was never so be-ryhmed since Pythagoras' time, that I was an Irish rat, which I could hardly remember.

Underlying these absurdities was the idea that animals were, when they did wrong, possessed by evil spirits, and also the crude idea of expiation, which made, until some time in Victoria's reign, of whatever killed a human being, horse, cart, locomotive, or what not, a deodand or forfeit to the King.

When Othello says (1, 3): "I will a round unvarnished tale deliver of my whole course of love; what drugs, what charms, what conjuration and what mighty magic—for such proceeding I am charged withal, I won his daughter," and having explained that "this is witchcraft I have used," he was making defense to an indictment framed in almost the exact words of the statute of 1603 (the date of the play is thought to be 1604), passed to please King James I, author in 1597 of a tract on demonology. This statute made it a capital crime without benefit of clergy to "use, practice, or exercise any witchcraft, enchantment, charm, or sorcery . . ." and also "to consult . . . entertain, fee or reward any evil or wicked spirit" for any purpose.

The *Suffolk Witches* case was tried in 1664 to the everlasting blot on the great name of Sir Matthew Hale, who charged the jury without expressing any opinion on the evidence, but stated his entire freedom from doubt as to the existence of witches. Our old friend Sir Thomas Browne, author of *Urn Burial*, testified at this trial as an expert; and the outcome, frequent when such gentlemen help confuse the ordinarily already befuddled jury, was a miscarriage of justice and in this instance the sending to their death of unfortunate old women. It took the courage and good sense of Lord Holt to stamp out this folly, by himself bringing about acquittals in all of the eleven witchcraft cases tried down to 1736 before him.

Othello was fortunate in the outcome of his trial. Conviction, followed by barbarous punishment, was much more frequent. Hero says to Beatrice (*Much Ado about Nothing*, III, 1): "If I were to speak, she would press me to death with wit." Nowadays if a defendant refuses to plead to an indictment, he is deemed to have pleaded not guilty and may die of old age before he is convicted, or his conviction is affirmed by the highest court. But formerly a defendant who stood mute had his refactory spirit broken—to say nothing of his bones—by punishment *peine forte et dure.* He was laid on his back and stripped of his shirt; heavy weights were piled on him and he was given dry bread and foul water "not from any fountain or river" until he answered, or was pressed to death.

"Attorneys are denied me," cries Bolingbroke in *Richard II.* His complaint was most unreasonable in view of the fact that an accused was not entitled to counsel, just as he could not, in this country previous to 1864, or in England until ten years ago, testify in his own behalf. So, too, when Buckingham was tried for treason in *Henry VIII* (II, 1), the treason having consisted chiefly in calling Wolsey a "butcher's cur," "The King's attorney urged on the examinations, proofs, confessions of diverse witnesses, which the Duke desired to have brought viva voce to his face." Vainly, for this ex parte procedure was following the usual custom of depriving the accused of what is now secured to him as a constitutional right, namely, opportunity to meet his accusers face to face.

In view of the frightful penalties that followed conviction of treason and the strong probability of conviction after indictment, one would suppose that the crime would not have been extended by implication. This was not the case, however. True, the indictment had to contain the word "traitorously," as Cade knew in charging Say with "traitorously . . . erecting a grammar school," but (*Richard III*, III, 5) ". . . Edward put to death a citizen only for saying, he would make his son Heir to the Crown; meaning, indeed, his house, which by the sign thereof, was termed so." This was a famous case, where the above words were construed as sufficient to constitute the crime of compassing the King's death.

"She is an adultress; I have said with whom; more she is a traitor" (*Winter's Tale*, III). The charge of adultery with Hermione, the Queen, was high treason for both. Henry VIII disposed of Anne Boleyn through this fiction. But when George IV brought Carolyn to public trial for adultery in 1820, he did not dare take advantage of the statute that made such act of the Queen high treason. Erskine demanded for her a definite charge and a list of witnesses before trial, and largely through his courage she was acquitted. It took the brilliant efforts of the same marvelous lawyer (who was so familiar with Shakespeare that he could carry on conversation on all subjects in the language of his characters) to acquit Lord George Gordon in 1781 of constructive high treason for wearing the badge of insurgents, on the theory that this was compassing the death of the King.

Not alone was criminal procedure harsh and cruel, but civil suits were scarcely less so. In the Epilogue to *Henry IV*, part 2, the dancer, referring to his previous promise of a better play, says: "I meant indeed to pay you with this; which if like an ill-venture it come unluckily home, I break, and you, my gentle creditors, lose. Here I promised you I would be, and here I commit my body to your mercies." He is referring to the early English bankruptcy laws that were inspired in modified terms by the privilege of creditors in the Twelve Tables to cut their delinquent debtor to pieces.

Imprisonment for debt is constantly referred to. In *Comedy of Errors* (IV, 2) Dromio of Syracuse says that "he is 'rested on the case," and in *Henry IV*, part 2, Falstaff, arrested at the suit of Dame Quickley, escapes by his wit, "being upon hasty employment in the King's affairs"; *Hamlet* (v, 2): "Had I but time—as this fell sergeant death, is strict in his arrest"; *As You Like It* (III, 1): ". . . make an extent upon his house and lands" (extent was a seizure of the person or chattels of a debtor as the initial proceeding in a suit); *Cymbeline* (III, 3): "A prison for debtor, that not dares to stride a limit" (persons arrested for debt were not allowed to go beyond certain prison bounds or limits; these in Ohio are coterminus with the county in which the debtor is arrested).

Deeds of land were long and solemn black-letter instruments. "The very conveyances of his lands will hardly lie in this box" (a coffin), says Hamlet (v, 1).

In connection with the descent of land, the legitimacy trial in *King John* (I, 1) affords instructive law. Only legitimate children (and this meant children born in wedlock) were "capable," that is, capable of inheriting.

> K. JOHN: *Sirrah, your brother is legitimate;*
>   *Your father's wife did after wedlock bear*
>   *him.*
> *And if she did play false, the fault was hers;*
>   *Which fault lies on the hazards of all husbands*
>   *That marry wives.*

This was sound law. All children born in wedlock were legitimate; nor could evidence to the contrary be received in a court of law. Even where a husband was beyond seas for three years, a child born a month before his return was declared legitimate in Y.B. 32 and 33, Edward I, 60 (1304), by Hengham, C.J., "because the private affairs of a man and his wife can not be known, for he may have come into the country by night before and begotten this child." The presumption was imperative that the husband was the father of his wife's children. Lord Campbell, around 1850, decided that a mulatto child with white parents having possibility of access was presumed legitimate. The foundation of the principle was the rule of policy charging a father with support and permitting the natural devolution of land, as laid down by Rickhill, J. (Y.B. 7, Henry IV, 9, 13 [1406]), "for who that bulleth my cow, the calf is mine." King John quotes this (I, 1).

One more illustration of the curious system of rules comprising the English law Shakespeare knew, and the sophistry with which it was argued. You are, of course, familiar with the grave diggers' scene in *Hamlet* (v, 1):

FIRST CLOWN: Is she to be buried in Christian burial that willfully seeks her own salvation?

SECOND CLOWN: I tell thee she is; the crowner hath sat on her, and finds it Christian burial.

FIRST CLOWN: How can that be, unless she drowned herself in her own defence?

SECOND CLOWN: Why, 'tis found so.

FIRST CLOWN: It must be "se offendendo"; it can not be else. For here lies the point: if I drown myself wittingly, it argues an act: and an act hath three branches; it is, to act, to do, to perform: argal, she drowned herself wittingly.

SECOND CLOWN: Nay, but hear you, goodman delver.

FIRST CLOWN: Give me leave. Here lies the water; good: here stands the man; good: if the man go to this water and drown himself, it is, will he, nill he, he goes; mark you that; but if the water come to him and drown him, he drowns not himself; argal, he that is not guilty of his own death shortens not his own life.

SECOND CLOWN: But is this law?

FIRST CLOWN: Ay, marry, is't; crowner's quest law.

This is satire on the unique case of *Hales v. Pettit*, published in Plowden's report some years before the first edition of Hamlet appeared. It shows a distressing example of how upright and fearless men have sometimes been persecuted for doing their duty. Hales, a puisne judge of the common pleas, had risked his life by refusing, at the close of the reign of Edward VI, to join in the scheme to set aside Mary from succession to the crown. Just after she had come to the throne, it became necessary for Hales to try certain persons who had been indicted for celebrating mass, contrary to the statutes of Henry VIII and Edward VI. The prisoners were found guilty, and Hales sentenced them. This brought upon him Mary's wrath, notwithstanding he had in the trial and sentence done only what according to the statute law he was obliged to do. He was removed from office and sent to the Fleet prison. There the tales told by his jailor of the tortures in store for such as were supposed to be hostile to the Pope unbalanced his mind, and when liberated from prison he drowned himself in a river near his house in Kent. The coroner's verdict, *felo de se*, or suicide, was most unjust. The poor man was no more capable of crime (which presumes intention) than was Ophelia. He did not receive Christian burial, however, and his body, with a stake driven through the breast, was buried in the crossroads as the law required. He had owned land in Kent in joint tenancy with his wife. For conviction of a capital

23

felony, such as murder or suicide, attainder was the penalty. Accordingly the crown conveyed this land as forfeit to one Pettit, who, entering upon it, was sued in trespass by Dame Hales. The narrow question in the case was: when was the felony complete? If at the time of the act resulting in death, then the land was forfeited, and she took nothing at the death of her husband; but, if at the time of death, then the land vested in widow Hales at that instant, and there was nothing for the attainder to operate upon. After most careful reasoning, in the course of which it was argued for the crown that the act is punishable, and that as the criminal is dead and beyond personal punishment, the only means of punishment is forfeiture of his goods and lands; and for Lady Hales that the act is not complete until death, it was solemnly resolved that Hales committed suicide in his lifetime when he threw himself into the water in which he drowned. The reasoning of the learned serjeants and of the judges who delivered the opinion is closely followed in the colloquy of the grave diggers; but it did not occur to our learned brethren, as it did to the "goodman delver" as a means of justifying Ophelia's Christian burial, that Hales did not drown himself, but that the water running down over him drowned him.

➤➤➤-➤➤➤-➤➤➤-➤➤➤-➤➤➤-➤➤➤◄◄◄-◄◄◄-◄◄◄-◄◄◄-◄◄◄-◄◄◄

Helen S. Trounstine Memorial
Meeting

(JANUARY 21, 1917)

This extraordinary, dear friend died at the age of twenty-seven. The range and vigor of her activities were almost unbelievable. Testimonials from eighteen different agencies, to which she had rendered brave and valuable services, were read during the exercises.

A RARE and notable life, spent among us, has been ended. But, though the visible existence of Helen Trounstine in this vale is, after short duration, terminated, the essence of her being has not descended into the grave.

She lived much less than half the days allotted in the Good Book to mortals; but if "we measure life by heart throbs," their intensity in effort and achievement, then, by that gauge, the earthly pilgrimage of our friend was not brief, but long.

It is altogether fitting that those who knew and loved her should now congregate to hear the facts and meaning of her life, the opinions of her associates, and the plan for enshrining in memory an example so illustrious. We owe this solemn duty to Helen, to ourselves, and to the great enterprises she championed with so much of valor

25

and fiery zeal. For if we will but be mindful of her qualities and be, by the remembrance of them, stimulated to further the causes dear to her, then she will continue to live in our every worthy act, in all high purpose and in each beautiful thought.

Stevenson, heroic sufferer, prayed for courage and gaiety and a quiet mind. Helen must have breathed the same prayer and it had been heard. She appeared, on the occasion of a visit to her shortly prior to her death, more tolerant than before. "Young, all lay in dispute; I shall know, being old." Preserving all her former enthusiasms, she was attracted to new interests as well. Thus, having lately learned something of proportional representation in city government, she was well impressed with the idea. In the course of a long talk, much of which amounted to argument, very keen on her part, because the subject was politics, and we were on opposite sides, she referred to herself not more than once or twice and in only the lightest and most casual way.

Now is it to be imagined that so indomitable a spirit has died? Of a certainty, if that will could thus overmatch bodily infirmity, that soul has vanquished death! There recurs to mind what is said of the passing of Ezra, at the close of *Daniel Deronda*:

> *"Nothing is here for tears; nothing to wail*
> *And knock the breast; no weakness, no con-*
> *tempt,*
> *Dispraise or blame; nothing but well and fair*
> *And what may quiet us in a death so noble."*

➤➤➤➤➤➤➤➤➤➤➤➤◄◄◄◄◄◄◄◄◄◄◄◄

Dedication of the Service Flag
of the University School
# of Cincinnati

(MAY 29, 1918)

*Mr. Seasongood's address is reprinted from the
school paper,* The Forge *(both the school and the
paper are no longer in existence). The speaker was,
at the time, a member of the Board, appointed by
the Secretary of War, to "Determine the Sincerity
of Conscientious Objectors."*

IN DEDICATING this flag and looking at the stars upon it,
one is led to inquire what manner of men are those
represented by these stars and what are the obligations
of the school in receiving this gift.

The stars symbolize some of the noblest and best who
have trod these halls. They are the St. Georges of today,
fighting the dragon of an absolute military despotism,
which would wither and destroy the world with its con-
suming breath of cynicism, hatred, and cruelty. They
are the Bayards, the Rolands, the King Arthurs, the
Sidneys, the Nathan Hales of this time. They are sancti-
fied! Their uniforms are the habiliments of righteousness. They are clad in the shining armor of a just cause.

"The rays of morn are on their white shields of expectation."

What a company they have gone to join! Let us recall to mind a few of that great concourse of heroes and saints—a few who will not return. And first, two poets.

Alan Seeger, before the war, was a young man twenty-five years of age, somewhat above the mediocre in poetic achievement. But the war made him aflame. He enlisted in the French Foreign Legion and wrote the deathless poems "Champagne," "I Have a Rendezvous with Death," and the "Ode to the American Volunteers Fallen in France." This last he was to have read before the statue of Lafayette in Paris, on Memorial Day of 1916. It was his threnody, indited in two days, while doing the hardest possible work in the trenches. He had what he craved, "that rare privilege of dying well," and how truly he proved:

> *One crowded hour of glorious life,*
> *Is worth an age without a name.*

His English prototype, Rupert Brooke, "a golden, young Apollo," of Rugby and Oxford, prior to 1914, was a master of versification, but the afflatus was not there. He had been something of a crank, much given to "isms." The great cause matured him swiftly. Returning from the Antwerp expedition and while preparing for the ill-fated Gallipoli campaign, in connection with which he died, on a French hospital ship in the Aegean, he gave utterance to those matchless sonnets, including that perfect poem of patriotism, "The Soldier":

If I should die, think only this of me:
That there's some corner of a foreign field
That is forever England. . . .

which will find a place in every Golden Treasury.

Then there is that great Hercules and Mercury, yes, that greater and better far than these, who ascended higher above the earth than Mt. Olympus, Victor Chapman, the first American to be killed flying for the Allies. About to take some oranges to a sick friend in the hospital, he spied a comrade, sore beset by a flock of enemy airplanes. He flew straight as a homing pigeon to the rescue and to certain death. His father, John J. Chapman, is a writer of distinction. But the father has been given literary immortality through the monograph, which forms the introduction to the collected letters of his boy. Read it, and your eyes will moisten and your heart will throb.

Now let your thoughts turn for a space to a great thinker, Donald Hankey, "A Student in Arms," "sublimely mild, a spirit without spot." His words have brought hope and solace to hundreds of thousands of the English-speaking world.

Some of these heroes were English, some American. Lionel de Jersey Harvard belongs to both countries. He was a direct descendent of a brother of the original John Harvard. He was a beautiful boy, with the features, brow, and curling hair of the Hermes of Praxiteles. He had one of those well-modulated, melodious English voices, and his words and thoughts were as lovely when, at the Harvard commencement of 1915, he spoke his message of love and good will. He had planned to be a physician and to war only on disease and death. He returned to England by the first steamer, to his beloved. He repeated to her the knightly words:

> *I could not love thee, dear, so much*
> *Loved I not honor more.*

He took his place in the trenches. Now, after three years of fighting, he is dead. He leaves an infant son to bear the honored name of Harvard, new honored after 300 years!

His contemporary at college, Harmon Craig, after receiving a mortal wound, was told one of his legs would have to be amputated. "Very well," he said, "I shall be able to dress quicker; one less shoestring to tie." Yes, he dressed quickly, he wears the robes of the angels.

I wonder if the widow of Lionel Harvard knows the widow of that other British officer, who inherits the Victoria Cross he won, for this: a grenade had been lobbed into a trench. It would explode and kill or maim fifty or a hundred men in that narrow passage. The officer fell on it, as boys fall on a football. His body was spattered over that trench, but not another man was hurt.

These deeds of valor are not done and these noble thoughts conceived alone by the officers and highly educated. Why, in a recent number of *L'Illustration* is a picture of a French sergeant, sixty-six years old, a volunteer, fighting in the first-line trenches? In his furrowed forehead one can see written "They shall not pass," as the law was written in the phylacteries on the temples of the patriarchs of old.

And you remember reading, last winter, how sailors

from one of our destroyers leaped into the icy waters of the North Atlantic to rescue a German sailor from the sinking submarine which would have assassinated their ship and done them to death.

Some names of the doers of deeds are known. Some deeds are known whereof the names of the doers are not known. How many deeds of nobility and sacrifice which will never be known, think you, have been wrought by the millions who sleep on the blood-soaked plains of Belgium and of France? We say of them the words of "The Song of Songs":

I am asleep, but my heart is awake.

Last week, one evening, the rain came down so fast it formed on the surface of the ground little waves, which were swept on by a great wind until they were stopped by a countergale and sank into the ground. These young lives are as those raindrops: they are driven in waves by the great winds of fate; they are stopped by undiscerning bullet and bayonet; they sink into the earth; but from them will grow much fine fruit and grain and many beautiful flowers.

How shall we garner these goodly crops; how make ourselves worthy to enjoy them? First, by letting the imagination be so roused that these great deeds and thoughts shall be known, although they never be told in the dispatches nor by the narrator of history. Then, having re-created these dreams of the dead, let those dreams become realities, through the living.

Let us be friends to all the great and good, even though we know them not. If Alan Seeger and Rupert Brooke have dropped the harp and the lute, do you, some here among you, now resolve that you will snatch them up and strike amain the harp and sound the soft notes of the lute; that you will write the poetry Alan Seeger and Rupert Brooke would have sung had they lived.

Oh, you will say, "That is the language of hyperbole. I am no poet. I know my limitations." Well, remember that Seeger and Brooke were not great poets before the war kindled the divine spark. Why cannot their lives and the war inspire you?

Is Victor Chapman's courage to die with his body? Take up his spear and hurl it at whatever is vile and base. Be a great politician, some one among you; be a great statesman and combat with Chapman's valor the political evils of your country, state, and city.

And shall Donald Hankey's gentle preachment reach only those hundreds of thousands who read his book? No! Hold high the torch he let fall. Consecrate yourselves, some of you, here, now, to become great preachers, priests, and rabbis, so that for years all within the sound of your voice and then their disciples may hear Hankey's dogma: the unimportance of creed and the fundamental value of the virtues of goodness and love of one's fellows.

Shall the sick be deprived of the ministrations of Lionel Harvard? Say no, with all the power of your being. Become a great physician. Do your own work and the work of Lionel Harvard, as well.

And that British officer—is his sacrifice to save only those, in that narrow defile, he shielded with his body? It must not be. He must be made to live again in your acts. You must work for the poor and unhappy; become, some of you, great toilers in the cause of charity. Why, you can make that British officer live again in as simple a thing as, when you see an infirmity or a deformity (and there will be many more than there are now), just appear not to see it and help the unfortunate one, without his being conscious of your assistance.

How often one hears the exclamation: "If only I could be in this fight!" There is no one of you who cannot be in this fight. I do not refer to actual military service, or to the work of the Red Cross, of the "Y," and of the other necessary activities in aid of the war. That you will assist with these is assumed.

What I mean is, you can help in the fight by ennobling your lives, by living the thoughts and deeds of the dead heroes, by so preparing for the period of reconstruction that the work of the warriors may be, in truth, fulfilled. If it is not, then a complete victory will not have been won, even should the allied armies march into Berlin.

This has been pointed out by no one more clearly than by Lieutenant Morize, of the First French Military Mission detailed to this country for the instruction of future officers. A graduate of the University of Paris, a former teacher at Johns Hopkins, bearing on his body two honorable wounds and wearing on his breast the *Croix de guerre*, he speaks with authority. He bids the students study diligently and not leave their studies until graduation. He likens the students to the reserves in the second-line trenches; they must be prepared and ready in the reconstruction period to attempt to take the places left vacant by many indispensable men.

So your studies take on new importance. In pursuing them, you have a part in the great struggle being fought for you. And this applies to the girls as well as to the boys. Women have had their opportunity through this war, and all they may accomplish, no one can divine.

Will the exaltation of a holy cause, the discipline and effectiveness learned in the army, the good relations between officer and men (so different from those between capital and labor), the disregard of station, riches, and creed, the promotion for merit alone, the unselfishness that is the root of courage, be preserved and carried into civil life? Much depends on you. You will be the companions, perhaps the helpmates of those who return. Your influence will be potent to determine whether they shall continue to lead the newer, glorious life or sink back to the humdrum existence of before.

Will the adjustment of war to peace conditions be accomplished with the least possible disturbance incident to a period of transition, or will the plowshare and pruning hook be so corroded that the nation will suffer a thousand times the anguish of the South after the Civil War? That will depend on you and the fitness of trained minds to grapple with new problems and to meet them with wisdom and patience.

Will there be a great, universal state, a league of nations, to make war forever impossible and to enthrone right supreme? Throw yourself on the altar of this noble cause. Then will you indeed have had a part in this greatest of all struggles, and then will this flag of service, of honor, and of love float proudly in the free air and stir the minds and quicken the hearts of all who gaze on its stars.

-»»-»»-»»-»»-»»-»»«-«-«-«-«-«-«

Julius Fleischmann as a Musician

(DECEMBER 15, 1918)

This talk was delivered at a civic dinner for the former mayor, who was leaving Cincinnati to reside in New York. While mayor, Murray Seasongood was ex officio a trustee of the Institute of Fine Arts and was active, though honorary, chairman of its drive for funds to support the symphony orchestra and to obtain what is now the Taft Museum.

PERHAPS you are wondering why the director pointed his baton at me for this solo. So am I. But a few days ago one of a committee appeared suddenly and said:

"We wish to ask you some questions. We have prepared to test your fitness to speak on this subject."

I replied: "*Andante a piacere*" (which, I need not explain to this company of victrola players, is the musical equivalent of "Go right ahead, as you please").

"Well, then"—he read the first question as follows—"which is your favorite sonata?"

"The Claro Perfecto," I rejoined, *un poco agitato*. "I like them mild. Frankly, however, I prefer the Partagas."

That should have satisfied him. But he asked a second question, namely: "Tell what you know of Scarlatti and Palestrina."

"As to the former, Scarlatti," I said *vivace*, "that is a catch question. This dinner is not for a great physician

3 5

like Dr. Christian Holmes, Fleischmann's brother-in-law, and I do not see what an Italian's pronunciation of the disease, scarlet, has to do with the matter. As to Palestrina, though, I can answer that: it is a mouth harp played by the inhabitants of the holy city when welcoming General Allenby."

"You will do," said the inquisitor. "I shan't ask you the remaining questions. No speaker I examined knows so much of his subject as do you of yours."

Having Rigoletto'd away from that overture, I proceeded to key myself up to getting in tune to string my subject, and learned that our tonight's guest is the truest and most considerate of musicians: he neither plays an instrument, or sings. But if he does not draw the bow for the violin, he excels in drawing the check for the violinist; and if he does not himself make the organ roll and peal, he is ever ready to peel the roll on behalf of the organist. He prefers gin fizz to Heifetz; takes lagers better than (Handel's) Largos, and the buffet better than the Buffa. He enjoys the symphony concerts vicariously, thinking with Keats: "Heard melodies are sweet, but those unheard are sweeter." Being vice-president of the May Festival Association, he is naturally happiest during the rest periods. In this, as in all things, he is at one with the great mass of Cincinnatians. Thus, enjoying the intermissions best, he is thoroughly conventional. Of the College of Music he is president in the most approved modern fashion—that is, *in absentia*.

"Why, then," we inquire, *doloroso*, "does he leave musical Cincinnati for New York? There all is Damrosch; here everything is Isaye. New York, it is true, boasts of Caruso, but Cincinnati still has a Zoological

Garden. Nevertheless, *lamentoso*, our guest has listened to New York's siren song entitled "Call Me, Malone." All we can do, therefore, is paraphrase Kipling's *Ballad of East and West* and say with a tremolo:

> *Oh, yeast is East*
> *And wets gone West*
> *And never on the train shall treat.*

So let us silence the trumpet, mute the strings, muffle the drums, sound the minor strain of the coda, and keep hoping for an occasional *da capo come prima*.

➤➤➤-➤➤➤-➤➤➤-➤➤➤-➤➤➤-➤➤◀◀◀-◀◀◀-◀◀◀-◀◀◀-◀◀◀-◀◀◀

Fifth Annual Exhibit of the
Duveneck (1848-1919) Society

(NOVEMBER 28, 1920)

His long interest in art, as demonstrated by his own collection of paintings and his role as an honorary life member of the Cincinnati Art Club, made Murray Seasongood the ideal choice for speaker at the opening of this exhibit at the Cincinnati Art Museum. The speaker was, for about thirty years, a member of the Board of Trustees and, for a number of these, vice-president and chairman of the Executive Committee of the museum and the art school. One of his talks shortly after his return from law school to Cincinnati was to the Municipal Art Society of Cincinnati on "The Importance of Beauty in Cities." In 1928, while chairman of the City Planning Commission, he introduced a resolution, which passed, to appropriate funds for a study of beautification of the Ohio River front.

*What needs my Shakespeare for his
      honored bones—
The labor of an age in piled stones?
Or that his hallowed relics should be hid
Under a star-y-pointing pyramid?*

38

Dear Son of memory, great heir of fame,
What needest thou such weak witness of
thy name?

Thou in our wonder and astonishment
Hast built thyself a livelong monument.

WHAT NEED of words is there for Frank Duveneck?
Happy is the artist whose life work becomes his visible
and enduring memorial. If you require a monument for
Sir Christopher Wren, look about you at St. Paul's; if for
Thorwaldsen, go to Copenhagen; and for Duveneck,
called by Sargent the greatest genius of the brush in
American art of his generation, look about you in this
room, at the collection left by him to the city he prized
and refused to desert. Only a few minutes ago Mr. Gest,
the director of the Art Museum, told me that the trustees
of the Chicago Art Museum at one time offered Duveneck a blank check, requesting him to fill in the amount
he would require to come to Chicago. He declined the
offer because he loved Cincinnati and wanted to remain
here.

Duveneck was a many sided man. He was a Cellini or
Da Vinci for versatility. But he was a great critic, as well
—something as rare, perhaps, as the great artist; how rare
may be judged from the fact that some of Duveneck's
greatest pictures sold originally for $25 or $100. Because
he was a great critic, he was able to help this museum acquire works which have enhanced in value some ten,
some a hundredfold.

But greatest of all, Duveneck was a friend. Of him

39

might be said what Charles Eliot Norton desired to have on his tomb:

He had many friends, whom he loved.

And because he was a friend, he had the spirit which made him a successful teacher. He was not like Themistocles, who could not sleep for thinking of the trophies of Miltiades. The triumphs of his pupils were his triumphs and their success was more a cause of happiness to him than his own. Hence it was that the "Duveneck Boys" gathered around him in Munich in the early seventies and became great names in American art—DeCamp, Alexander, Twachtman, Chase, to mention a few—and now this society whose fifth annual exhibit opens today honors him and itself by adopting his name. At this moment, too, there is an exhibit in New York of works of "Duveneck and his Circle."

When Duveneck died, the idea that his teaching should not end with physical mortality immediately came into the minds of his pupils. Spontaneously, without organized effort, it was understood by all that his work must be carried on, and the Duveneck fund began to grow, some of his pupils contributing fifty cents and some $500. Then the art clubs of the city contributed their mite, among them the Cincinnati Art Club, the Woman's Art Club, the Art Department of the Woman's Club, the Ceramic Club, the Crafters Company, and today there was contributed by one donor $5,000, so that the total fund is now about $20,000. It is desired to raise $125,000 or $150,000, the income of which shall be used to augment the salaries of those teaching at the academy, perhaps to assist in developing other Duvenecks. A group here has volunteered to assist in raising this fund; and should we not all contribute as Duveneck would have done, not to match what one's neighbor gives, but each according to his ability in evidence of affectionate remembrance of the great master?

Duveneck fashioned, with our own Barnhorn, the statue of the Seer of Concord, at Harvard College. Emerson's words in encouragement of American art recur to mind:

Let statue, picture, park and hall,
Ballad, flag and festival,
The past restore, the day adorn,
And make tomorrow a new morn.

-»»-»»-»»-»»-»»-»»«««-«««-«««-«««-«««-«««-

8

Commencement Address to the
Milwaukee Country Day School

(JUNE 8, 1921)

Murray Seasongood had recently served two terms as chairman of the Schools Committee of the Associated Harvard Clubs.

JAMES RUSSELL LOWELL said that after-dinner speeches should contain an anecdote, a platitude, and an idea. A good many such I have heard make up for the absence of an idea by at least two platitudes. No one, so far as I know, has, however, prescribed what a standard commencement address should be. In some to which I have seemed to listen, a wordly wise person addressed advice to persons not particularly anxious to hear it. I suppose a commencement address may be a species of lay sermon of a not too solemn character. This combination is difficult, reminding me of a friend who was offered $100 apiece for a series of talks, provided he would come to the place of performance in an airplane. He replied: "If you want an orator, get Bryan, and if you want a flier, get Rickenbacker. But you can't get both an orator and a flier for a hundred dollars."

I congratulate you boys who have finished your school course and are ready to become college men. I congratulate you on having this new terrain open to you and hope you will approach it with the idea that commencement from college is but the beginning of learning; or, as I heard it recently expressed at a college commencement: "Now that you have acquired your A.B., go and learn the rest of Alphabet." I felicitate some of you upon your prospective attendance at Harvard. The years you will spend there should be among your happiest. If I may make some suggestions, they are:

Saturate yourselves with the spirit of the place and get the inspiration from thinking you are attending a college almost 300 years old, the college of, for example, Adams, Everett, Roosevelt, Longfellow, Emerson, Agassiz, Gray, Child, Lowell, Norton. I have no wish to detract from other places; there is glory for all. But there is inspiration and the incentive to a higher resolve, if you will get the feeling of tradition, of almost three centuries there of learning, friendship, and public service.

Lowell also said: "A University is a place in which to learn things that are not useful." By this, I think he meant that the principal benefit of university training is to acquire a love of scholarship and of learning. This does not mean necessarily accumulation of knowledge of a practical character, but rather the desire to study and gain capacity for intellectual enjoyment through one's whole life. A mistake is to elect at college only courses of practical benefit, believing study of cultural branches can be made after graduation. For, when you have got out of the quiet of the Yard into the workaday affairs of life and its heavy responsibilities, you will find it increasingly difficult, both because of pressure of other matters and because of consequent unwillingness to study, to enter

43

new fields of investigation. Still a matter of regret to me is that I did not take William James's course on metaphysics or Kittredge's Shakespeare; and it is one of my lasting satisfactions to remember Shaler's geology and Norton's fine arts, neither of which, so far as I am concerned, has been of the slightest practical benefit, unless there is a benefit of thinking better on your particular life work by reason of having thought on subjects unrelated to it. The great Harvard Law School professor John Chipman Gray, an authority on some of the most difficult subjects in the law of real property, including the rule against perpetuities and restraints on alienation, had his son, now also a brilliant lawyer, prepare for his chosen profession of law by devoting himself, in college, almost exclusively to classics. This is perhaps not a fair example of the wisdom of studying the nonessential, because in the law one of the most important things is a nice appreciation of the meaning of words, and this can more readily be attained through knowledge of the classics.

Of equal importance, however, to your studies of books should be your acquaintance with men. Ruskin said of Norton: "He had a talent for friendship." There is no talent that can afford greater happiness. "There are as many uses for friendship as for fire and water." Cicero said of it: ". . . there is nothing which . . . is so exactly what we want in prosperity or adversity." Here, I believe, is one of the great advantages of a nationally recruited student body: you come in contact with men from all sections of the country and, at Harvard, from other sections of the globe, as well. You will perhaps be chilled at first a little by a certain New England reserve, which seems strange to persons who have grown up in the approachable atmosphere of the West, Middlewest, and South. It is a survival, perhaps, of Puritan sternness and of the long struggle of the New Englander with a rocky soil and dour climate. But here again the national character of Harvard is of advantage to New England. Successive generations of New England men have been subjected to the warmth and cordiality of men from other sections of the country, and the reserve at first encountered is very soon dispelled. Particularly is this true now, as all freshmen are housed in the wonderful freshmen dormitories. Here all classes are thrown all together. Friendly freshman-house competitions bring the freshmen together as a class, free from the interposition of upperclassmen and clubs, all of which have pledged themselves to leave the freshmen to themselves, and with the most abundant opportunity to develop friendships. These last for the balance of college and, indeed, for life. Do not believe anyone who may tell you that this is a rich men's college: a very large proportion of the students are working their way through college, and no man is discredited for doing so. There is no college where a man receives more recognition for what he is, regardless of wealth, position, or whence he originates. Coming from a distance, you have a certain advantage in selection of companions, not being tied up too closely with a group on entering, as is the case if you had come from some eastern school. Your choice is as broad as the class, almost as the university.

One of the great values in college friendships is that lapse of years is of no moment in them. "Friendship abolishes time." You may not see one another for years, and yet when you meet, you resume where you left off. No friendships you will have are so pure, unselfish, and enduring as those you will make at college. Another benefit is, you may come to wish to be what your friends think you.

Now what are you to do with the love of learning and the talent for friendship you are to acquire? Not use them for your own enjoyment, but realize you have been greatly blessed and that you are expected to use what you have acquired for the benefit of others. After you leave the academic enclave, you will find many evils, against which you should break a lance, much that is badly done, and much not done at all. We pride ourselves on being an educated people, but statistics brought out by the war and subsequently show that the lack of even elementary learning among large numbers of our people is appalling. While it is not true as stated by Machiavelli: "There is no sin but ignorance," it is a fact that ignorance is one of the most fruitful causes of sin.

Resolve now that these great years on which you are to enter will be marked by preparation for a life of usefulness to your community and country and love of your fellow men.

➤➤➤➤➤➤➤➤➤➤➤➤➤➤◀◀◀◀◀◀◀◀◀◀◀◀◀

Tarbell's Portrait of
Professor Samuel Williston

(JUNE 15, 1922)

This speech is reprinted from the Harvard Alumni
Bulletin, *Vol. 25, No. 17 (Jan. 25, 1923), p. 478.*
Mr. Seasongood was a member of the Council of
the Association and also served as its vice-president.
During portions of 1947 and 1948 he was visiting
professor of law, teaching municipal corporations at
the School, and from 1951 to 1953 he held office as
the first president of the Cincinnati Harvard Law
School Association.

IF THIS were a first-year class, I should be very much
tempted to ask whether, assuming a person bought a new
suit to wear when making an address and the train is an
hour late and prevents him from rigging himself up in
style, he has an action against the railroad. For this assembly, however, that question would not be difficult of
solution.

In presenting to the school the portraits of those who
have helped to make it illustrious, the Council of the
Harvard Law School Association considers that it is rendering a valuable service. These canvases overcome mortality and strengthen tradition. To those denied the
privilege of direct contact with the masters is afforded

the inspiration of seeing their features and expression and of being reminded that this is a school at which these great men taught. This portrait of Professor Williston seems to me admirable. One can almost see the twinkle in his eye, as if he were elucidating the "smoke ball" case, or one of the others. Just as we, when students, were thrilled by the portraits of Story, Greenleaf, Washburn, and Parsons, and reminded by their pictured images that they had taught in this school, so those who follow, in the years to come, will look at these canvases and be stimulated, their enthusiasm will be quickened, by seeing the features of the pioneer Langdell, the chivalrous Ames, the elemental Gray, the Thayers, father and son, seer and martyr (for such the younger truly was), the kindly Smith, and now this latest addition, and, we hope, many of his colleagues who will be added to the group.

A great poet, who may also have been something of a lawyer, admonished that to "gild refined gold and to paint the lily—these things are excess." And so one might think, at first blush, it is likewise superfluous to speak in praise of a dear and revered instructor in this company, among whom, I believe, more than half are his pupils. However, the counter thought to that idea has not been expressed better than by the president of this Association, Mr. Justice Holmes, who said, on the occasion of the death of F. W. Maitland: "When praise comes after the master's work is finished, then it is too late for that encouragement which all require and of which the successful get too little." Therefore, if what is spoken here should cause Professor Williston embarrassment, that embarrassment will yield, I think, to his enjoying another tribute of loyalty and affection from his pupils.

The Harvard Law School Association and Professor Williston are old friends. Thirty-five years ago when still a student in the school, he obtained a prize from the association for the best essay, his subject being "The Law of Business Corporations before 1800." In the generation that has gone by he has amply justified that award, in the triune capacities of legal author, draftsman, and teacher.

As legal author—the courts quote his books as authorities of the greatest eminence and weight. His publishers, in their prospectus of the great work on *Contracts*, in 1920, state they regard it as the crowning achievement of one hundred years of publishing law books, and a lawyer wrote them in reply that that was a very proper statement on their part, and he believed that for the next one hundred years they would have great difficulty in finding a crown nearly so good.

As legal draftsman, he complies with the formula of Stephen, that legislation should be so clear it may not be misunderstood even by minds desirous of reading it in bad faith. You may be interested to know how the Uniform Sales Law was enacted in at least one eastern state. It was through a classmate of mine at the Law School who, by the way, was almost denied entrance because, already an older man, he told Dean Ames he intended not to practice law, but merely to study. That man got to be a great political power in his own State of Rhode Island and when the Uniform Sales Law was presented, he said to the committee having it in charge: "It is not necessary for you to read this law; you probably would not understand it if you did; it is not important that you should. I say to you, my teacher, Professor Williston, who is the greatest authority on Sales that ever lived, wrote this law and my advice to you is to pass it just as it is." The advice prevailed.

But, as Professor Williston wrote in his letter to our treasurer when informed he was to be asked to sit for his portrait, the major portion of his life has been devoted to teaching, and in that he has rendered his most signal service. His influence as a teacher is incalculable; it has spread to all the various sections of this country and to other countries. No man who has studied with him but will be more open-minded, more frank with the court, more generous to his adversary, more enamored of our mistress, the Law, by reason of having sat at the feet of this wise, patient, just, pleasant man, than he would otherwise have been. If I may refer again to words of Mr. Justice Holmes: "Most of the education men get from others is moral, not intellectual." "Men learn from the specialists that bustle and push are not the equal of quiet genius and serene master." "If a man is great himself, he makes others believe in greatness; he makes them incapable of mean ideals and of easy self-satisfaction."

The tutor of Sir Philip Sidney desired there be inscribed on his monument only the fact that he had been the tutor of Sir Philip Sidney. The pupils of Professor Williston are content if it be recorded of them that they were his pupils and followed his precept and example.

➤➤➤-➤➤➤-➤➤➤-➤➤➤-➤➤➤-➤➤➤◄◄◄-◄◄◄-◄◄◄-◄◄◄-◄◄◄-◄◄◄

10

"The Shot Heard Round the Wards"

(OCTOBER 9, 1923)

Mr. Seasongood's talk at the Cincinnatus Association, unexpectedly printed in the next morning's newspapers, originated the movement for an amended charter that was adopted by the voters in 1924. Good government under it began January 1, 1926, following the election in November 1925 by the voters of Cincinnati, of a council of nine at large by the nonpartisan Hare System of proportional representation method of voting. Mr. Seasongood was one of the founders of the Cincinnatus Association, and served as vice-president and chairman of its Program Committee. In 1924 he was one of six originators of the "Birdless Ballot League" (object: to vote for men, not birds), which became the City Charter Committee, and for a time was chairman of the Executive Committee, as well as one of the three drafters of the amended charter.

As toastmaster a few years ago, the former mayor, in introducing Mayor Briscoe of Dublin, observed: "The Mayor in Ireland is addressed as 'Lord Mayor,' or 'Your Worship'; here as 'Your Honor,' or sometimes 'You're another.' You, sir, are given the magnificent gold chain of office, which we see you wearing tonight hung around your neck; here, not infrequently, the retiring mayor has hung on him an appendage of baser metal."

Regarding Mr. Seasongood as mayor, see "Our American Mayors: xv. Murray Seasongood of Cincinnati," by Russell Wilson, associate editor of the Cincinnati Times-Star, *in the* National Municipal Review, *Vol.* xviii, *No. 2 (Feb. 1929); also "Liberating a City: How Cincinnati Cleaned House, a comprehensive story of how Cincinnati's impotent majority achieved expression," by Silas Bent,* The Century Magazine *(1926), pp. 303–13.*

THEY TELL YOU at the City Hall that they have no money for this, no money for that. What I want to know is, what becomes of the money?

Another excuse is that the county receives more than its just share of the taxes. There is no excuse in that. The city and county are run by the same gang.

It is not so much the extra taxes we pay that I object to; it is the moral and psychological effect which this machine is working upon the citizens of Cincinnati.

In what other city in the country does the administration place the payment of dividends to a public-service corporation before the just payment of a franchise tax? You cannot find one. But here in Cincinnati we charitably postpone and then eventually wipe out what the Traction Company owes the city because it must pay dividends to the stockholders, not only of its own company, but of holding companies as well.

What is to come of the rapid-transit plan? Ask anyone on the street, and he will shrug his shoulders. Ask the officials of the city. They do not know.

We have the fourth largest per-capita expenditure of

any city in the country. What do we get for it? Nothing, absolutely nothing! We have the only occupational tax of any city in Ohio. What becomes of that money, and how much is collected under that system? Nobody seems to know.

In what city in the country would the people tolerate the passage of a gas-rate ordinance on the orders of a political boss 600 miles away, after members of the City Council had refused to enact it? We do in Cincinnati, even after the order is given wide publicity by the press.

Why are our streets in such bad condition? Read the specifications on which the contracts are let. They are perfect. If they were followed, the streets would be good for years. On the street I live, Washington Avenue, we formed a committee to see that all the conditions in the specifications were carried out. The street is as good as it was twenty years ago.

Another point. If the county gets more than its just share of the taxes, what does it do with what it receives? Recently the county commissioners attempted to spend something like a quarter of a million dollars to purchase unauthentic records of deeds. They are not good as evidence in court, and every attorney knows that. Why did the county commissioners find it so important to have those records?

Another thing I object to as a citizen of this community is the fact that the common-pleas judges of this county, in whom are vested the power to appoint trustees of the Southern Railroad and who are supposed to exercise all their judicial knowledge and impartiality in determining the fitness of anyone considered for the position, wait for the Hamilton County Executive Commit-

53

tee, which is only another name for the leader who lives in New York, to make its recommendation, and the judges immediately concur in what amounts to the appointment by him.

In addition to the taxes, there is a cold half-million of rental derived yearly from the Cincinnati Southern Railroad. In figuring receipts, this amount is somehow left out in the computation.

When a person calls at the City Hall to ask for an improvement, he is sorrowfully shown the condition of the building, the dirty windows, leaky roof, and dirty walls.

All that is beside the issue. Look to the big things. Street repairs; sewage system; nonpayment of franchise taxes by the Traction Company; a wallow of expenditure in building "a hole in the ground," popularly known as the proposed rapid-transit plan—that is where the money goes, and it is time for the citizens to assert themselves.

I for one believe the time has come to cut out every extra tax levy, bond issue, or anything else that will give this bunch a chance to squander money. Make them produce results on what they have or get out.

The whole history of the organization has been a blot on the city. As far back as 1905 it was known that the political leader here demanded of the three judges of the Court of Appeals, then the District Court, that they reverse a decision in favor of the city for $280,000 against a large contracting firm. Two of the three did so, and were re-elected; one refused, and was not re-elected.

Yet for twenty years we have gone on supinely indifferent to our welfare, ready at all times to swallow whatever the gang put before us.

54

Some may say that 1905 is ancient history so far as the affairs of the city are concerned. But the same gang is in power; and less than two years later a certain official, now a leader, overnight produced $214,000 when, as treasurer, he was threatened with indictment for converting that amount to his own use from the taxpayers' money.

I do not know where a copy of the report on the affairs of 1905 can be found, but if it can be found, I should like to make compulsory that every member of this association read it. It gives a wonderful insight into how our city is run.

It is criminal what the people of Cincinnati are undergoing, not only in receiving nothing for their money, but in being drugged into a state of political lethargy that is fast making the city a place of derision.

11

The Cincinnati Real Estate Board

(NOVEMBER 1, 1923)

*This talk was given during Murray Seasongood's
solo campaign against the Republican organization.*

WHEN I went to school (I really did go to school once),
I used to think that the feat of Horatius holding the
bridge and Leonidas holding the pass at Thermopylæ
were considerable accomplishments. For the past month,
however, since I have been attempting to withstand the
onrushes of the gentleman from New York and his co-
horts, I have come to the conclusion the task must have
been rather simple, if the character of the attack on
those historic occasions was similar to that here. I am
now of opinion that the severity of an attack does not
necessarily depend upon numbers and that, in certain
instances, the more there are, the more they interfere
with one another and the easier resistance is made.

Apparently, I have been selected as a kind of Arnold
Winkelried for the spears of the office-holders. I am entirely willing this should be so, as long as the spears are
hurled in the daytime and not below the chest. I say to
them in the words of Scott:

> *Come one, come all! this rock shall fly
> From its firm base as soon as I.*

An orchestrion is an instrument played by one person and sounds as if it were a complete orchestra. The "sounding brass" of the campaign manager's trombone, the "sweet complaining grievance" of the mayor's violin, the high, sharp notes of the editor of an afternoon paper's piccolo, all played by the master at the keyboard, Hynicka, are music to my ears. However, certain parts of the orchestra have not yet had their solo. I, therefore, call for the sheriff's double bass and the city engineer's percussion to complete the harmony.

First, as to the sheriff, the county commissioners by agreement with the sheriff pay him sixty-five cents per prisoner per day. The United States government pays him seventy cents a day per prisoner. The city, I believe, pays him the same for its prisoners as the county pays. From these three sources he received for the year ending March 31, 1923, approximately $70,000. Why should the sheriff personally from this one item (remember, whatever is saved in the county could be utilized by co-operation toward the relief of the city) apparently receive from $15,000 to $25,000 a year profit at the expense of the county and city on keep of prisoners? I say *apparently* because I do not know certainly. I await further information from the sheriff. . . .

It has been stated that I am a political partisan. If I am, I am a partisan Republican. I voted for our late President, which cannot be said of the New York head of the local organization in the national convention. The vote on the extra levy has resolved itself into the question: do the citizens of Cincinnati and Hamilton County like what has been done by those in power or do they disapprove? If they like what they have received, let them vote for the extra levy. If they wish to show their disapproval and their emphatic insistence on efficiency and economy, let them cast their ballot against the extra levy.

England Our Friend

(JULY 1924)

*The first meeting of the American Bar Association
in London provided the occasion for this speech,
which was delivered by Mr. Seasongood aboard the
S.S.* Laconia, *one of three vessels booked principally
by lawyers and their families to attend this event.
The address is reprinted from Mr. Seasongood's article "The A.B.A. in London: 1924 and 1957 Compared," in the* Ohio Law Reporter *(Dec. 30, 1957),
p. 45. For his amusing log of this sailing, see the*
American Bar Association Journal, *Vol. 10, No. 9
(Sept. 1924), p. 667.*

"I HATE that man," said the gentle Charles Lamb, whose
birthplace near the Temple in London we are soon to
visit. "Why," replied a friend, "you don't even know
him." "That's it," stammered Lamb. "If—if I knew
him . . . I couldn't hate him."

And is it not so with nations? Lack of understanding
often is the trouble. From visits such as this we may
expect a better acquaintance that will deracinate those
erstwhile, almost national pastimes of plucking the ea-
gle's feathers and twisting the lion's tail. . . .

At Guildford, an Assize town and county seat of
Surrey, still stands the ancient Castle Keep to which
King John, after signing the Magna Carta at Runny-

mede, repaired and suffered those awful pains, whether of remorse or from overindulgence in lampreys is still a matter of historical dispute. At Edgeborough School, in Guildford, I learned some thirty years ago the truth of what Thackeray quotes in an essay: "A German, in imperfect English, queried of an Englishman: 'What do you make (do) in your schools?' the reply was: 'We make men in our schools.' Men, indeed, they are, whether from "public" or other schools, as evidenced by the ribbons and decorations of our officers and crew; men of courage and steadfastness in war, and of fairness, self-restraint, and achievement in the arts of peace.

Last summer my wife and I sauntered into the Central Criminal Court. There, with no other introduction than my name and "member of the bar of the U.S.A." scribbled on a piece of paper (I had no card), Mr. Under-sheriff Deighton, a solicitor of distinction, appeared and showed us around. He pointed out in one of the court-rooms the son of Charles Dickens, Mr. Common Serjeant Dickens, presiding. A little alert, perky old man of seventy-four, he conducted his court as if, having read *Bleak House*, he had resolved that Mr. Tulkinghorn should have no place there. We heard, in another room, the recorder, Sir Ernest Wilde, taking pleas of guilty. He embodied the spirit of the great chancellor for whom Shakespeare's Wolsey had wished: "May he . . . do justice for truth's sake and his conscience; that his bones, when he has run his course and sleeps in blessings, may have a flood of orphans' tears wept on them."

What impressed me was the fairness of the proceedings. The Scotland Yard officers had a record of the prisoner's life. They and the barrister prosecuting would emphasize the good points as much as the bad, and the counsel who appeared for the defense would as frankly admit bad as good. It was an approximation of justice that kindled enthusiasm for like endeavor on our part. "Do you know why they strew herbs on the floor and each judge has a nosegay?" asked the undersheriff. "It is a survival of the Great Plague of 1660. The herbs were thought to have a medicinal value and the judges held flowers to their noses to prevent getting the prevalent stench and infection. During the war, there were those who would have abolished these long observed practices as useless expense. But, we decided to adhere to the custom."

"*Nolumus leges Angliae Mutari*," said the Lords on a famous occasion. But last month the Legitimacy bill passed its first reading overwhelmingly in the House of Commons. So we see, too, in retrospect, Chief Justice Holt laughing out of court trials for witchcraft; the great figure Lord Mansfield declaring that no human being can be a slave on the free soil of England; Lord Brougham "of every human right a champion, of every wrong an avenger." So, in the sweep of memory, the Reform bills pass. We behold the House of Lords shorn of its power of veto, and great estates returned to the common domain. With the Boer War over, behold, in South Africa the late Dr. Jamison, as legislative leader of the opposition, speaking in English and outvoted by a Boer majority in Dutch, and General Smuts, the former foe, becoming a great English general; the woman's suffrage question settled; and then a solution, perhaps temporary, of the comparatively simple Irish question; and now a first Labor cabinet with important members, Lords

Parmoor and Haldane. The ability of England to preserve tradition and yet adapt itself to new and changing conditions is one of its glories. Our Concord wise man, Emerson, counseled: "To have a friend, be one." Let us be friends of the British people whose hospitable shores we approach.

꘍꘍꘍꘍꘍꘍꘍꘍꘍꘍꘍꘍

13

The Avondale School

(OCTOBER 27, 1925)

*In this address, Murray Seasongood was urging the
election of the Charter Party Council.*

THIS IS the birthday anniversary of a great American,
Theodore Roosevelt. Let us be glad such a man lived
and gave his strength to the betterment of government;
and let us cherish his memory in grateful remembrance.
Let us hope, too, that November 3 will be for this city a
day of congratulation and of a new freedom.

In the recent meeting of Mr. Hynicka with his cla-
quers and supes, the precinct workers, the *Enquirer* says
I was referred to as a "loud speaker and chanticleer."

Perhaps I am a loud speaker, but it is necessary to be
such to make my opponents running for office—and my
gracious, how they are running (away)—hear me; because they will not get on the platform with our candidates, but content themselves with whispering slan-
ders which cannot be checked or refuted. Well, if I am
a loud speaker, I am right here and it is not necessary to
get in touch with New York or California to hear what
I have to say. As to chanticleer, our opponents simply
will not recognize that we are dealing with a birdless
ballot. Chanticleer, in the play, tried to protect his fam-

63

ily and neighbors from the buzzard, and so the characterization is not inapposite.

Mr. Hynicka still shouts for party regularity. What has he to say of party irregularity in the person of the late clerk of the municipal court?

Every branch of the public service is demoralized under the present system. Take, for instance, the sheriff. It is his duty to gather up stray dogs. That "disgruntled band of reformers," the Academy of Medicine, have twice stated in the most positive terms that the present epidemic of rabies is due to his nonperformance of this office. I suppose the children who were bitten by mad dogs which the sheriff failed to collect were Democrats and allowed themselves to be killed purely for "political propaganda."

But if the sheriff cannot collect dogs, he certainly can collect excess charges for feeding city prisoners. No wonder we have not sufficient policemen. The organization state platform took cognizance of this graft and promised to remedy it, but, of course, nothing has been done.

Mr. Hynicka says he stands on the Upson Report (an organization-sponsored survey of government in the city and county). If so, he is likely to fall; for this report, which was signed by one of his present candidates for council (Adolph Kummer), besides calling attention to the profit made by the sheriff, says of council:

> *Ward representatives in the very nature of things are likely to overemphasize the requirements of their localities to the detriment of the city as a whole, and we think the evidence is clear that this has been done in the past.*

Truly, as the sheriff is Witt, the council is humor, or rather tragedy, with the surveyor saying: "The great majority are mere voting automata."

If Hynicka stands on this same report, this is very hard on one of his candidates for council (Schneller), because the report says distinctly that the city clerk's office is overmanned and extravagant. The committee, including one of the candidates who is running, says of his fellow candidate, in his official capacity:

The report on clerk of council shows that his staff could be cut down materially with resultant saving.

This same candidate, after an open primary had been promised President Harding, threw his ward, the eighteenth, so hard for Wood that there was practically not a Harding vote in it.

What reliance can be placed on any promise they make?

→»→»→»→»→»→»«←«←«←«←«←«←

14

Last Speech before Election

(1925)

*A short excerpt from Mr. Seasongood's speech for a
Charter Party Administration.*

A FRIEND who is a great traveler recently told me of a
striking similarity in the government of Constantinople
and that of Cincinnati, as it has been administered. I
knew we were in the same latitude, but I had not realized
before that we had sunk to the same depth. Stray dogs
roam the streets there in large numbers, and the streets
are full of holes. On one day each year, however, the
Sultan rides from his palace to the treasury. In preparation for that day, all the dogs are kept off the streets over
which he rides, and the holes are filled up to make his
transit comparatively safe. In a few days thereafter, the
dogs are again at large and the streets are again full of
holes.

Successful Charter Candidates

(DECEMBER 31, 1925)

The Cincinnati Times-Star quoted the remarks made at this luncheon tendered successful charter candidates by Republican organization opponents. See Murray Seasongood's "Forms of Municipal Government in the United States," in the Municipal Review of Canada, Vol. XL, No. 10 (Oct. 1944), p. 12; The Shire & Municipal Record of Sydney, Australia (May 28, 1944), p. 43; also, reprinted with comments and questions for students in "The Practice of Exposition," by Joseph M. Bachelor and Harold L. Haley. In addition to the "great advantage" resulting from proportional representation listed below, an additional advantage of that system is set out in a portion (not printed in this volume) of "Local Government in the United States: A Challenge and an Opportunity," Lecture IV, p. 110, as follows:

Second, where the minority concur, as they did in almost all enactments in the early years of the Charter government, and one of their number in Council was leader of the Republican machine, they cannot be heard and are estopped to complain of what was done with their full knowledge and concurrence.

As to the proportional-representation system of voting, see Seasongood: "The Merits of Proportional

Representation in City Elections," in Social Science,
Vol. 16, No. 3 (July 1941), p. 237.
*This system continued to be the linchpin of the
good-government wagon in Cincinnati until, following several unsuccessful attempts at repeal, it was,
unfortunately, removed by a majority of the voters
in 1957.*

WHILE I regret that all of the Charter Committee candidates could not have been elected, I feel that a great
advantage of the charter is that it cannot put one side
completely in power. . . . It is helpful to the council
itself to realize, as Sir Roger de Coverley observed, that
"much may be said on both sides." If you have a critical
minority, you know before you do an unwise thing what
will be said against you for doing it, and this makes you
more reasonable in your course of action and you reach
a more judicious conclusion. It is much better to have
adverse criticism before a step is taken and so avoid it,
than to take the step and learn, when it is too late, it was
a bad one.

Citizens Party Dinner

(JULY 26, 1926)

*Murray Seasongood gave this address in the cam-
paign for the election of nonpartisan reform candidates in county offices, and was an originator of this
movement. Some of the Citizens' achievements are
detailed in his Lecture* II, *"County Government,"
in* Local Government in the United States: A Challenge and an Opportunity," *pp. 44–63. For more
information about this movement, see Mr. Seasongood's chapters on Robert Heuck (Citizen County
Recorder and Auditor) in* The American Politician
(*Chapel Hill: University of North Carolina Press;
1938*) *and Chapter 24 on John Bricker in* Public
Men In and Out of Office (*id.; 1945*), *both edited
by J. T. Salter.*

Now AS TO the prosecutor and the sheriff and gambling
in the county, and particularly gambling at Coney Island.
Why all this pother now? What has opened the sheriff's
eyes and roused the prosecutor from slumber? The Coney
Island Race Track operated all last summer, undisturbed.
Can anyone rationally say that the race-track gambling
scandal of last summer was not due to the sheriff's and
the prosecutor's nonperformance of duty, and that that
nonperformance was unrelated to the interest of Hynicka
and Schott in Coney Island? If they had been in earnest,
why could not the test case they initiated just before the

primary election this year have been begun and completed at the opening of the track last year? In the Civil War, "smooth-bore" was the name for imitation cannon planted on forts to deceive the enemy. The prosecutor and the sheriff, in their friendly present attack on Coney Island, are nothing but "smooth-bores." They are making a great noise and pretense of action, whereas if they had been in earnest, gambling would not now be going on at the track, and the retail merchants and other creditors would not be clamoring for relief against loss and defalcation. . . .

Now, I understand, I am expected to be a kind of civic gladiator, always ready for a fight, and so to take cognizance of the gentle castigations and weekly bilge water emitted from the Strand Building.

So far as concerns myself, I intend to take no notice of the "slings and arrows of outrageous journalism." I have cultivated the disease known as ichthyosis, which gives one a hardening of the skin without internal disturbance. I am having the time of my life. My assertions of the past three years are being proved true; we are accomplishing things in Cincinnati to its lasting benefit. It will never lapse to where it was before this movement was begun, and so I repeat the couplet:

> *Sticks and stones will break my bones*
> *But names will never hurt me*

and grin at headlines such as: MAYOR MISLEADS WOMEN VOTERS.

But the malevolence and mendacity of this sheet toward the city administration are worthy of notice; first, as showing the low character of the Hynicka leadership and, second, its plain hostility to a successful city administration although predominantly Republican. The Hynicka paper states that it is published by the "Republican County Central Committee." Its object is to advance the candidacy of the Hynicka organization candidates. They must take responsibility for its attitude, which is one of blind hostility to the city government and the city manager. Privately a number of the Hynicka candidates have come to the city manager and to me and said they disapprove of this paper and consider it both untruthful and stupid. But they do not dare make such expressions publicly, and if they make such objections at all to the publishers, it shows the truth of what we assert, namely, that the candidates themselves are mere lay figures under the Hynicka system, and the actual planning and work are done by the boss.

➤➤➤-➤➤-➤➤-➤➤-➤➤-➤➤《《-《《-《《-《《-《《-《《

17

Mayor's Address

(JULY 26, 1926)

*Murray Seasongood delivered this talk at the cere-
monies preceding the demolition of a historic hotel
for the erection of a large insurance building on the
site. It is reprinted from a pamphlet, containing all
addresses, entitled "The Burnet House (1850–
1926)."*

THIS IS an unusually pleasant day for me because the
president has told me I am to have some of the flowers
here to take home, and, I assure you, it is a very unusual
experience for a Mayor, while still alive, to receive
flowers.

When the president referred to P. T. Barnum as having been a guest at the Burnet House, that recalled to me
an anecdote told of him. When he was ill, he said to the
attending physician: "Doctor, what are my chances?"
and the medical attendant replied: "Mr. Barnum, you
have the greatest show on earth."

Well, President Sage had one of the greatest shows on
earth this morning in the old Burnet House, and I am
sorry that all who are here, and many others, could not
have been there to see the great historic personages
marching for the last time down the grand stairway.

You have perhaps heard of the old lady who said to

Mr. Lecky, the historian: "I do not read history, because I believe in letting bygones be bygones." The chairman has more vision than that, because he realizes that history is experience and creates tradition, and that tradition is more potent than laws and is what we have sorely lacked in our American cities. Many businessmen would have said only: "Put on the wreckers." In making the demolition of this venerable structure, so intimately connected with Cincinnati's growth, an historic occasion, the chairman has shown vision and imagination and given an earnest that the affairs of the company are in wise hands.

Dr. Goss, in his history of Cincinnati, says that when the Burnet House was opened in 1850, it was, with its 340 rooms, the finest hotel in the country and perhaps in the world.

As the chairman has said, the Burnet House is of special interest to me for a reason I shall mention. I feel as if I go a good ways back myself, and am almost like the man who could remember Lincoln before—and Columbus after—supper, because the father of the Jeremiah Smith who recently returned to Hungary the proffered gift of $100,000 for untangling its finances (and if Louis Kossuth smiled this morning as he marched down the stairs, he had good reason for doing so) was one of my teachers at the Law School, and his father fought in the Revolutionary War.

The Burnet House is one of my earliest childhood recollections, because the place of business of my father, uncle, and great uncle was immediately opposite, at the southwest corner of Third and Vine streets, and the hotel, with its large lobby, seemed to me a magnificent

73

structure. An uncle of mine, of advanced years, tells me he remembers seeing General Scott there when the General returned from the Mexican War. Mr. Nathan Park informed me this morning, in the hotel, that he remembers having heard Garfield speak there, and another friend told me how vividly he remembers having seen swarthy Logan and Blaine there during their campaign.

Of course, the story of Charles B. Wilby, when a little boy, working his way through the crowd from the front steps to get close to Lincoln as he spoke, and how Lincoln referred to him and placed his hand on his head, is familiar to all of us.

But, as William James says in his great book, "A condition of remembering is forgetting." So, likewise, a condition of progress is destruction, and because a nobler structure is to supplant the one that has now outlived its purposes, no sadness need attend its razing.

Let us take inspiration and resolve so to do our part in this city we love that when our mortal habitation crumbles, our accomplishment will live on and make better and happier those who take our places.

➤➤➤➤➤➤➤➤➤➤➤➤➤◀◀◀◀◀◀◀◀◀◀◀◀◀

18

Mass Meeting in Atlanta

(MAY 12, 1927)

Mr. Seasongood addressed himself to the citizens of Atlanta, Georgia, in the city auditorium at Taft Hall.

I CANNOT say too much for the city-manager form of government. One branch of it, often unnoticed, is particularly important: that is, the separation of the ceremonial and administrative duties of the mayor under the Federal form plan. It is tremendously burdensome, if not impossible, for one man to perform both of these duties, and the council-manager form of government recognizes this fact and leaves the city manager free to attend the administrative duties, and imposes the ceremonial and political duties on the mayor. This is as it should be for another reason: namely, that the mayor is elected by the council after having been elected by the people and so is really elected by the people. Fears of tsarism should therefore be dispelled, because the people can get rid of the mayor by the simple expedient of not voting for him for council.

The ceremonial duties are important in that they provide a contact between the city administration and the electorate. It is most important that the city officials should be able to present their problems to their constituents and that the citizens should have a ready means of presenting suggestions and grievances.

It is said of Mayor Walker, of New York City (how truly I do not know), that substantially all of his time is devoted to the ceremonial duties of his position, and I can readily believe this is so, because I have, in our comparatively small inland city, made more than 200 talks of various kinds in less than a year and a half that I have been in office, with no signs of respite for myself and hearers for the future.

Relieved of ceremonial and similar duties, the city manager may devote himself continuously to the administrative and business end of the government, having full opportunity for planning years in advance and not exposing himself to the necessity of taking sides or of being misunderstood in what he may say.

I have been told that there is some little apprehension here that the women, who are sponsoring the proposed charter so actively, may control the government. I do not see why that should be a misfortune, if it should happen, as they control us in our homes, anyway, and do the job tolerably well. However, in these matters an ounce of experience is worth a pound of theorizing. I can say that the women in Cincinnati are largely responsible for the government under which we are operating, and they have been thoroughly unselfish about it, not even aspiring to positions as women and effacing themselves as candidates in the forthcoming election.

You are particularly fortunate in your proposed charter in that by Section 55 you have boards serving without compensation, whose duty is only to consult and advise, but not to direct. In Cincinnati, while we have independent nonpaid boards, who have rendered distinguished and unselfish service to the city and who have the entire confidence of our citizens, we also have a so-called Rapid Transit Board, which, appointed before our administration, in my opinion is the worst board that ever boarded at a city's expense. I mention this board as a survivor of the form and kind of government we had before adopting the present one.

Under our charter, we have the somewhat anomalous situation of the nonpaid boards, to which I have referred, being appointed by the mayor with the advice and consent of council. Theoretically, this might be an interference with the administrative end, but we have been most fortunate in getting the highest class of citizens to serve on these boards, and one good effect of having them appointed by the mayor is that it keeps the city manager from, with each appointment, making, as a former president said, "One ingrate and one hundred enemies."

Perhaps the greatest advantage of the council-manager form of government is concentration of responsibility. It is the greatest mistake imaginable to suppose that all the work in the city-manager government is done by the city manager. He cannot function unless he has a mayor and council who will carry out the spirit of the charter. The determination of policies is wholly in them, and when the council is truly representative of the best citizenship, the council is not overshadowed by the city manager, because people realize that the policy-determining is done by the mayor or the council and they are responsible to the electors for the results.

➤➤➤-➤➤➤-➤➤➤-➤➤➤-➤➤-➤➤-➤➤-➤➤≺-≺≺-≺≺-≺≺-≺≺-≺≺

Dr. David Philipson's Fortieth
Anniversary

(NOVEMBER 3, 1928)

*Mr. Seasongood gave this address in honor of Dr.
Philipson's fortieth year as rabbi with the congregation of Bene Israel in Cincinnati. It is reprinted
from pp. 40–3 of the brochure descriptive of the
event.*

I RISE to speak with considerable discomfiture. Who
would not, when the musical selection just preceding
was "Come away, come away"? One gets somewhat
used to this kind of thing, however. Recently the music
before my address was "How long, O Lord," and as soon
as I finished, "Now praise be to God."

I have not sufficient Biblical learning to remember
anything appropriate to forty years. I recall reading that
at the time of the great flood, there was rain for forty
days and forty nights; also, that the children of Israel
wandered in the desert forty years. With every attempted
ingenuity, I cannot make these references germane, since
the children of K. K. Bene Israel have had forty years in
a spiritual land of Canaan, a land of religious milk and
honey, under their beloved Moses whose forty years of
spiritual leadership we celebrate tonight.

Dr. Philipson is, for me, not merely a man, but an institution. "He has been a lamp unto my feet and a light unto my path." Why, he even induced me once to teach the graduate class in his Sunday School. I used his work, *The Jew in English Fiction,* as a textbook, with great pleasure to myself, whatever the pupils may have thought of their instruction. In many of the most solemn occasions of my life, Dr. Philipson has had a part. As a reminder of my Sunday school days, I have a prize book inscribed by him. My brother was in his first confirmation class. I recited the confession when I was confirmed, almost forty years ago. My wife and I were married by Dr. Philipson. He officiated at the burial services of my father—and for how many others has he performed similar rites in joy and in sorrow, "like the shadow of a great rock in a weary land."

Dr. Philipson is a many sided man. He does not remain secluded in the Holy of Holies. To multitudes has he said: "I shall light a candle of understanding in thine heart which shall not be put out." He has interpreted the calling of the priesthood broadly and, therefore, he is a great citizen as well as a great rabbi. He has interested himself in such outside activities as the Young Men's Mercantile Library Association, the Literary Club, the Americanization Committee, the Associated Charities, and many others. "A wise man is strong; yea, a man of knowledge increaseth strength."

But it is to Dr. Philipson as a citizen that I should like to devote a few words. There are some who maintain that a preacher or rabbi should not discuss topics of the day or matters that are controversial. Dr. Philipson has not taken that view, but rather the text: "As the ruler of the city is, so are all they that dwell therein." (Of course, that is pretty hard on Cincinnati at the present time, but it appears in the selection Dr. Philipson usually assigns me to read on Yom Kippur.) Our rabbi regards citizenship and the fearless discharge of civic duty as a religious obligation. Thus, as far back as 1898 (thirty years ago), we find him urging the doing away with sore spots on the city's surface, and calling attention to the fact that Cincinnati then had less park space than any large city in the country, a condition which has now, fortunately, been remedied.

In 1900 he protested vigorously against the efforts of Boss Cox to take away home rule from the city of Cincinnati—now guaranteed by our Ohio Constitution.

In 1904 he made a stirring address before the graduates of the University of Cincinnati. He urged them to vote "against the boss, for clean streets, for more and better cars, for better schools, to stop gambling, for clean officials."

In 1908 he helped found the Honest Elections Committee. He called "traitors in times of peace" those "who deliberately and in cold blood plan to corrupt the ballot and steal by this foul means victories at the polls which would otherwise never be theirs. These traitors lower the colors of American citizenship to the dust. That which should be priceless they make a thing of barter and sale."

Again, in 1909, he did not hesitate to announce how he would vote in the municipal election and why. In his travels he was "forced to hear from keen observers that Cincinnati is losing ground in every way. This condition is due to the fact that this city for over a score of years has been under the thumb of an iniquitous political machine."

In 1911 he quoted from the Prophet Isaiah against corrupt judges, those "who decree unrighteous decrees to turn aside the needy from justice." This was at a time when certain local judges admitted having been called to Boss Cox's office and asked by him to decide against the City of Cincinnati a case pending.

This seed has fallen on good ground. All thanks to Dr. Philipson, who, in many long years of hardship and discouragement, with real courage, fought the fight for betterment of our municipal government.

There is another characteristic of our beloved rabbi to which I should like to make brief reference. It is his open-mindedness to new ideas. "Hostility to youth is the surest sign of age." According to this, Dr. Philipson is young, notwithstanding his forty years of service in our midst (although I think I detected in him tonight at dinner the first sign of age when, recalling his advent to this city, he said I was then a very pretty boy). I have always found him receptive and considerate of younger men. He let me preach a homily in his pulpit not long ago on "A Layman's View of Religion," and the next week commented, with perfect good nature and fairness, on the suggestions contained in it, finding some worthy of adoption and others not. His is Lord Mansfield's toast, "Old books and young friends," with old amities as well.

Dr. Philipson is so catholic (or should I say Jewish?) that he will not object to my closing with a quotation from a pagan: "Late mayest thou return to Heaven," or, as we express the wish, may it be long "before the silver cord be loosed and the golden bowl broken." May he go from strength to strength; may the spirit of the Lord rest upon him, "the spirit of wisdom and understanding, the spirit of counsel and might; the spirit of knowledge and the fear of the Lord," Amen.

❯❯❯-❯❯❯-❯❯❯-❯❯❯-❯❯❯-❯❯❯❮❮❮-❮❮❮-❮❮❮-❮❮❮-❮❮❮-❮❮❮

20

Ohio River Dedicatory Celebration

(OCTOBER 22, 1929)

The annual convention of the Ohio Valley Improvement Association attended the dedication of a new system of navigation dams on the Ohio River, and a thirty-foot granite shaft situated high on a bluff in Eden Park, overlooking the river. Mr. Seasongood's welcoming address to President Herbert Hoover is in the printed pamphlet record of the proceedings, pp. 95–7. In 1932 he was a member of the President's Housing Conference, Section of Slums and Blighted Areas, and, with co-authors Newman F. Baker and Lawrence Veiller, submitted a paper: "Some Legal Aspects of the Slum Problem," Appendix I, pp. 14–26 of the Report of the Committee on Slums and Blighted Areas.

THE VISIT to this city of the country's Chief Executive is a matter of happiness for all of its inhabitants. Usually such a visit is in connection with some important occasion, as, for example, when John Quincy Adams, then former President, came here, in November 1843, to assist at the dedication of the first municipal observatory.

Your visit, too, Mr. President, is not only a joyous occasion for our citizens, but will ever mark the completion of a great federal project of tremendous importance to this city, and who can say to how many other regions.

83

A great warrior used to complain that he was much subjected to literary persons, and I have no doubt, Mr. President, that you are much subjected to welcoming speeches containing weary statistics intended to show the importance of the local community. Probably, however, as the State of California is proud to claim you as one of its citizens, you have become, in a measure, used to addresses of welcome delivered in no apologetic tone.

Accordingly, may I mention that you are in a city somewhat unique in our American municipalities; in fact, the business of the city is conducted as any great private business is conducted. The Merit System is genuine and is not used as a means of keeping out of positions persons politically undesirable, or as a means of getting into positions and keeping there those desired for vote-getting strength. We do not regard it as of importance what the views of our street sweepers are on the League of Nations or the protective tariff. Here efficiency and service are the tests that govern the electors in making their choices of officials to conduct the public business. At the same time, the citizens of Cincinnati are keenly interested in the national parties; and their independence of them in local affairs has not injured, but on the contrary has strengthened these parties; as, relieved of troublesome questions of patronage, they may devote themselves to their real objects, the discussion of principle. This is shown by a tremendous increase in registration this year for a purely municipal election, and an overwhelming vote in presidential years for President and Congressmen according to the normal national political belief in this community.

"The Queen of the West in her garlands dressed, on the banks of the beautiful river" welcomes you wholeheartedly, Mr. President, expresses its pride in your distinguished achievements, and trusts that you will speedily return for a much longer stay.

➤➤➤-➤➤➤-➤➤➤-➤➤➤-➤➤➤-➤➤➤-≪≪≪-≪≪≪-≪≪≪-≪≪≪-≪≪≪-≪≪≪

21

The Challenge of Youth to the Synagogue

(JANUARY 17–21, 1931)

Mr. Seasongood's topic was part of a symposium on "The Synagogue and Its Relation to Modern Thought and Life," held by the XXXII Council of the Union of American Hebrew Congregations in Philadelphia.

I FEEL very much honored to have been given the opportunity to speak on the subject "The Challenge of Youth to the Synagogue" for several reasons. It implies in the first place that I have some intimate knowledge of the synagogue and that I am not like Charles Lamb, whose hostility to clergymen was such that when asked to say grace at a dinner, he looked furtively up and down the banquet board and exclaimed: "Are there no clergymen here? . . . Thank God."

I suspect that the real reason why I have been given this subject is because there is a challenge in it. In my home bailiwick I am regarded, much against my inclination, as rather a bellicose individual. I fear people think of me as of the man defending himself in court, to whom the judge said: "You may challenge any of the jurors," and after looking over the panel, he replied: "I'll fight that little fellow in the corner." All I can say is, that if

Israel's message is peace, for the past five years I certainly have been an apostate.

Well, then: exactly what is youth? And has a portly, middle-aged person past fifty the right to speak for youth? You may remember that Emerson, upon being congratulated on his seventieth birthday, said: "I count it a melancholy day; it is the end of youth." And of course one of the best definitions of genius with which I am familiar is that which describes it as translating the feelings of youth into the experience of age.

Certainly I agree that "crabbed age and youth cannot live together," but I think that the emphasis should be on *crabbed* age, and I see no inconsistency and no difficulty about age as such living with youth and getting along very well.

We who are interested in affairs of the synagogue must remember that in Holy Writ it is said: "Your young men shall see visions and your old men shall dream dreams."

An observation I wish to make is that in my experience there isn't anything the matter with youth. Youth is all right. I feel that human nature doesn't differ; it is a constant factor. The manifestations of human nature in different ages are different, but human nature is the same year in, year out, and century in, century out.

And another thing I think we should take into consideration is that this idea that youth is the happiest time of life is a mistake. I don't consider it to have been so. My youth was very happy, and yet youth is bound to be a time of stress and struggle, and so far as I am concerned, I am a great deal happier now, having arrived at whatever I am, than I was in a period of discontent in some instances, of first becoming aware that there was such a thing as injustice. When you first become cognizant of that, you cannot sleep at night. And I suppose it is one of the penalties of coming old age that later you remember that injustice has existed at all times and in all ages; and it doesn't interfere so much with your nightly slumbers. But the younger person certainly has a period of stress. He thinks about what his career is going to be, he thinks of whether he is going to be a success, he thinks if he will marry and what the outcome of that will be. And so I have a feeling that it is a great deal better to have arrived at middle age or older, even if you are a failure, than to have the troublesome queries and endure the uncertainties that arise in the mind of youth.

Now the subject assigned to me is "The Challenge of Youth to the Synagogue," but we must delimit this subject. It might with almost equal meaning and propriety be "The Challenge of the Postwar Age to Religion in General, and Particularly to Religious Worship," for attendance at religious worship in the past decade has shown a tendency to diminish. This is of course an age of transition, to be compared with the change from the tool to the machine age. And as in all such ages, persons then living are often the sufferers by reason of changes. We read about them in histories in an impersonal way, we read of the period following the Civil War, we read of the postwar period, but they were all individual human beings who lived in those periods, and our consideration of this problem must have that factor in mind. Man's, and even more, of course, woman's horizon and interests have expanded. You will recall the description in Proverbs, Chapter 31:

A woman of valor who can find?
For her price is far above rubies.

Now that is a conception of woman somewhat removed from her ordinary activities of present-day life.
If woman's place is the home, as has been said, she may
feel that there is no place like home for her. I do not
repeat that at all in adverse criticism: I think she is
perfectly right. There are new activities in which she may
engage and show her ability and her equality with the
male sex. I mention it merely to call attention to something I am sure must be in your mind: that the sphere,
the horizon of woman in thought and action has been
greatly enlarged.

Certainly there is less rigid observance of the Sabbath
in these days. There is a far greater opportunity for
secular education. It has been said that our colleges to
some extent have pushed the parson off the pedestal.
But certainly there is a greater opportunity for knowledge. It isn't necessary to get knowledge alone in the
synagogue, as might have been the case when opportunities for education were not general.

Again, denominational loyalty and schisms no longer
have the intense significance they once had. That is not
different in our religion than it is in Christianity. Here is
an excerpt from *The Revolt of Youth*, which was kindly
furnished me by one of the rabbis:

Christianity is on trial throughout the world of
youth. There is a widespread faith in Jesus, but lit-
tle belief in the organized expression of his spirit.
In many places the church is blamed for the World

8 9

*War. There is a revolt against formalism, against
orthodoxy, against competitive divisions in the
Christian ranks, with considerable disgust with the
superficialities which consume so large a share of
the church.*

*The religion of youth is mystical, often pantheis-
tic, and unorganized, but it is based upon the will
of the individual man to find his way to God and
worship him without the restraints of dogma as he
sees fit*

—a viewpoint expressed long ago by Frederick the Great,
when he said: "Let every man go to heaven in his own
way." I think our people get weary of internal dissentions
in Judaism. They don't like these controversies between
the Orthodox and the Reform Jews, and they don't like
the bitterness with which a question of fact is attacked to
determine some question between the Zionists and the
anti-Zionists. All that they feel not to be ideal religion,
but against it; and they wish and aspire to a more complete unity.

The mechanical changes of this century have revolu-
tionized pursuits, and naturally, as an accompaniment,
habits of thought. This is no more true of Jews than it is
of non-Jews, nor true of the youth more than it is of
people generally in their relations to religious worship.

Well, now, there are certain adjustments in this
changing world of ours, in this period of transition and
flux, which should be made if religion is to retain its hold
on the interest and enthusiasm of the young people.
Youth resents dogmatism. Our religion cannot longer
rely on its *ipse dixit*. It cannot say: "This is written in a

book, and this book has become sacred, and that is all there is to it; you are not supposed to think, you are supposed to accept." Youth will not, in this age of criticism and questioning and independence, tolerate such a position if it is assumed by the synagogue, and the only effect of it will be that youth will avoid the synagogue and leave it to older persons in which to submit to dogma.

The attitude toward youth should be: "We don't know it all, let's try to reason this thing out together; let's see if we can present a solution for your difficulties which we know exist; and we don't approach it with the idea of dictation, in a compulsory spirit. Let us explore jointly whether there is a real utility inhering in the synagogue as conducted."

Second: youth finds a great deal of complaint—I say youth, but I think some of the older people have the same objection—because of the inordinate length of the service. The age of the three-volume novel and of the hour or more sermon is past. All life has been speeded up. Our young people are used to the automobile, the radio, and the motion pictures, and all three move fast. If you have a critical young person sitting there subjected to what Shakespeare would term "damnable iteration," the constant repetition over and over again of supplicatory prayers, this young person is very apt to become impatient and irreligious. Young persons are not impressed with that kind of thing, and they are apt to say: "Why, you are just like Charles James Fox, who said that an argument repeated twelve times is as good as twelve arguments. If you are undertaking to supplicate the Lord, why isn't it enough to say it once and be through with it, and if He hasn't heard or heeded you, then the fact that you keep on repeating it isn't going to make any impression."

Third: young persons must be allowed greater participation in the ceremonies of the synagogue. They don't like just to sit and be preached at, they don't like to have nothing to do with the service at all. I think there must be many of them who, when they hear a hired choir, sigh: "Why don't we have a choir of our own? Why don't you let us be the choir? Maybe we won't sing as well, maybe the organ will not be played as well, but all spiritual devotion gets to God, and He will make allowances for our insufficiencies, and for our youth." What they desire and what they feel they are entitled to is participation in the service as, for example, by being the choir or by getting up and singing hymns. There is a satisfaction in standing after a long time and singing. It is partly physical and partly spiritual, too, in expressing oneself in some way and not be sitting there for hours and be talked to and preached to and to hear prayers and have nothing but a passive interest in what is going on.

Young people say: "Isn't there an inconsistency in hortatory and supplicatory prayers? In one breath you say: 'Here is an omniscient God,' and then proceed to imitate the preacher who said: 'We don't mean to dictate, O Lord, but merely to suggest.'" They say there is an inconsistency in the kind of prayer which on the one hand speaks of an all-wise, right-determining Being, and on the other hand ventures to ask Him favors for His creatures; and if they are to have any part in it, they want to have it themselves and not to have their work done for them. So, all the ceremonial occasions should give greater opportunity for participation by the young people and by all persons in the synagogue.

And what is going to be the result if that participation isn't allowed? The same thing that is happening in the colleges. You find a great deal of complaint on the part of a number of persons that the extracurricular activities in contradistinction to the classroom passivities are the more attractive. Some undergraduates are more interested in the outside activities at college than in the scholarship for which college is supposed to exist.

And so you find among our young people a tremendous interest in charitable work, you find a great interest in the brotherhoods and the sisterhoods and the centers—in all things where they have opportunities of self-expression and where they feel that they are an essential part of what is going on; and if you don't allow the young people to be active in the ritual of the synagogue, they will drift off into these extra synagogue activities and interest themselves more in things that are not directly akin to the synagogue.

We had a Jewish welfare-fund drive in Cincinnati recently, and it was one of the most extraordinary and inspiring sights to see the number of young people who would come out day after day with enthusiasm and delight and pride in their work. This was one of the most heartening things that I have ever seen in a Jewish community, and it was because they were doing something positive and active, and not being told about the eternal verities and what was good for them.

Finally, the rabbi must be a person of real, first-rate

93

ability. He must be a spiritual person in his life, he must be a pastor as well as a great thinker and a great orator, because he is in competition with persons who are of that kind. It is perfectly feasible for a person now who wants religious refreshment to listen to some of the great preachers of this country over the radio; and if the rabbis are to retain their hold, they must be men of the character that I have indicated, in order to retain the interest and enthusiasm of the young people who are just as able to hear that kind of a superior person as they are to go to the synagogue and hear a person of mediocre attainments.

And again, the rabbi must speak on matters that are of vital concern, matters that are going on at the time. It has been a reproach to churches that in times gone by, some of the greatest movements for humanity have received no encouragement, have been met only with silence in the pulpit. Those will occur to you, many of them. I don't know, when human slavery existed, whether it was customary for the rabbis or preachers to lift their voices and proclaim that that kind of a thing was a sin and that it ought to be done away with. All the talk about creed and about schisms and things of that kind seems inconsequential to a young person in comparison with stirring questions, such as how to eliminate sordid and corrupt government in the Republic and in its local subdivisions. Young people are interested in those things, they want to hear something about them, they want encouragement and assistance to combat those evils. They want to know about the prevention of war, they want to know about industrial questions and the present overwhelming problem of unemployment, the better dissemination of truth through the press, and what are legitimate changes to be made in the moral code, which is satisfactory enough to us older people who have grown up with it, but which isn't entirely satisfactory to them; or at least which they wish to inquire about, in the spirit of young people who are critical and troubled and in a difficult and unsettled world.

I haven't the least doubt that youth wants religion. They need it, they are concerned over this unsettled state of affairs, they are disturbed by fault-finding with the moral code that many of them learned. They want to know if this code is right, or if it isn't. Some want solace for troubled and wounded hearts, and the place that they wish to seek it and help is in places of worship. And it is not rash to prophesy that they will cling to the places of worship, if religion will adapt itself to the necessities of an age of change and of questioning.

⇥⇥⇥⇥⇥⇥⇥⇥⇥⇤⇤⇤⇤⇤⇤⇤

22

Godkin Lectures at Harvard

(1932)

Reprinted from Murray Seasongood's book, Local Government in the United States: A Challenge and an Opportunity *(Cambridge: Harvard University Press; 1933). The excerpts used here are from: Lecture* I, *"City Government—Cincinnati," pp. 12–13;* II, *"County Government—Hamilton (Cincinnati) County," pp. 38–9;* III, *"Hindrances to Good Local Government," pp. 68, 87–9, 92;* IV, *"Helps," pp. 93–5, 101–2, 120–1;* V, *"Changing Views—The Remedy," pp. 134–7.*

In 1938 Mr. Seasongood addressed the Harvard Summer School on "The Press and Local Government" (printed in part in the Boston Transcript, July 15, 1938). For his article respecting himself and the Cincinnati press, see the Nieman Reports, July 1947. The speaker served as a consultant in 1937 and as a member of the Overseers Committee to Visit the Graduate School of Public Administration at Harvard from 1940 to 1947; also, from 1944 to 1947, as a member of the Committee to Visit the Department of Government, and again from 1958 onward.

LECTURE I

City Government—Cincinnati

ONE OF the great objects in life should be to attempt to reap some good from calamity.

Sweet are the uses of adversity,
Which, like the toad, ugly and venomous,
Wears yet a precious jewel in his head.

The yield to be gleaned from this period of sorrow and want is the recognition of the importance of local government, and of the fact that the best way to reduce taxes is to have competent government in the cities and counties of this country. The emphasis has been heretofore on savings in national and to some extent in state government, but the amounts spent on local administration far exceed the sum of the state and national expenditures. The debased public morality that made possible for so many years in this country the rule of Tweed, Croker, Kelly, and Murphy of New York; McLaughlin of Brooklyn; McManes, Durham, and Vare of Philadelphia; Magee and Flinn of Pittsburgh; Butler of St. Louis; Cox and Hynicka of Cincinnati; Lundin, Sullivan, and Thompson of Chicago; Behrman of New Orleans; Ames of Minneapolis; and Ruef of San Francisco has not aroused the capacity for sustained indignation and effort which should long since have swept aside the despoilers of our cities. Well, then, if the moral nature of our people has not been sufficiently stirred to make such outrages impossible, let the depleted purse accomplish the same result. Let people understand that poor local government is extremely costly to them, whether they pay direct taxes or only the cost of taxes borne by the landlord and the purveyor; that millions of dollars of tax money can be saved by efficient local government, which can be obtained, howbeit with difficulty. Then this long period of calamity and suffering will not have been in vain.

We in Cincinnati do not need to philosophize about these matters. We know what can be accomplished from the experience of our own community.

LECTURE II

County Government—Hamilton (Cincinnati) County

MOORFIELD STOREY, delivering the Godkin Lectures in 1920, quoted Carl Schurz as follows: "If Gabriel draws your charter and Lucifer administers it, your government will be bad. If Lucifer draws your charter and Gabriel is called upon to administer it, your government will be good." I venture to add a corollary to this striking statement. It is: "If Gabriel draws your charter and Lucifer administers it, your government will be better than if Lucifer also draws your charter."

In other words, Pope's "For forms of government let fools contest" is not entirely accurate. Form of government is not decisive, as respects either good or bad local government, but it is important. Cincinnati and Hamilton County, in which it lies, offer interesting evidences of the truth of this assertion. The charter adopted in Cincinnati is an excellent form of government, and has greatly aided in the success achieved. Hamilton County has this country's usual form of county government, the worst possible, decentralized and lacking administrative control, with numerous elective officials wholly independent of one another. And yet good government obtains there, despite it. Manchester, England, has a council of 140 members. There is a loosely organized system of departmental committees, with the city clerk as the only central administrative head; the system works because trained and experienced department heads are appointed.

It has been estimated that government of all kinds costs from ten to thirteen billion dollars a year in America. Local government, as distinguished from state and national government, spends more than fifty per cent of the sum, whatever it is. From 1922 to 1932 New York City's budget grew from $326,000,000 to $615,000,000. There are at least 140,000 persons on that city's payroll. It is apparent, therefore, that amelioration in form and performance of local government are of real importance to the taxpayer.

The Republican organization used to treat the Courthouse and City Hall as its property. At election time elevators were plastered with cards of the machine candidates, and opposition cards, if placed by the temerarious, disappeared after one trip. On election day these buildings were practically deserted, because most of the employees were ward and precinct executives and had to be at the polls or doing political work all day—and indeed for days and weeks before election. The merit system did not exist; it was evaded by the specious pretext of calling numerous employees deputies, no matter how ministerial their work. A small ring of favored contractors had virtually all of the public contracts. A certain attorney received pay for his services on the unusual basis of half a cent a gallon for tar and a cent a yard for crushed stone going into county roads. Newspaper editors testified in one of the legislative investigations before referred to that they paid the sheriff one third of the fees received by them for public advertising in foreclosure and partition cases. The sheriff was made a per-diem allowance greatly in excess of cost for prisoners fed by him in the county jail, and no accounting was given or asked respecting the excess. Other examples of looting the public treasury could be extended indefinitely.

None of these conditions exists now in Citizen offices. A complete Merit System is being installed as fast as possible. The Citizen office-holders did not indiscriminately discharge all employees who had opposed their election; they realized that the men were not to blame for the system, and in numerous instances retained efficient employees, exacting only the promise that they would refrain from partisan activity, surrender their machine positions, and do their work loyally and impartially. Many were glad to do this, and justified the faith reposed in them.

Our people must interest themselves in reasonable econ omies, and the result will be that without curtailment of necessary services, taxes will come down. Cincinnati and Hamilton County Charter and Citizen movements for good government have prevailed in eight of the last nine annual elections, and from their successes, moral results aside, the people have derived benefits and savings amounting to millions of dollars.

The possibilities of other material economies in county government are very numerous.

There is nothing peculiar in the victories gained in Cincinnati which makes them impossible of attainment in other large cities of the country, if citizens there will be resolute, unafraid, moderately self-sacrificing, and united in a determination that right shall prevail.

LECTURE III

Hindrances to Good Local Government

THE OBSTACLES to good government in our cities and counties are grievous, and in many localities appear, even to those fairly desirous of obtaining better administration, insurmountable. The picture is gloomy, sordid, and discouraging, and I wish we might overlook it and turn at once to the reverse side of the medal, the helps and encouragements to progress. But if we are to advance, we must appraise some of the principal causes of our national degradation, and inquire which are, in truth, ills that we must bear. We should adopt something of the attitude of General Goethals, when building the Panama Canal: his subordinates would outline to him engineering difficulties, showing in great detail why a certain thing could not be accomplished, and he would reply: "All right! Now that you have given me the reasons why it cannot be done, go and do it."

Local gangs are injurious aside from the questions of patronage which take so much time and effort of the appointing official, because they intensify indifference and keep many a citizen away from the polls in despair. There is a great deal of clamor about the failure of citizens to vote, but often those loudest in deploring it are silent as to one of its most substantial causes.

The indifference of the ordinary citizen to the local affairs of his community has grievous consequences. It leads to ignorance of what is going on, and of what may be accomplished by reasonable effort. So there has grown up a considerable body of opinion which cynically wishes government to be incompetent because, ridiculous as the argument seems, it fears that if government is efficient, it will encroach more and more on private enterprise. This attitude, as was well observed recently by Professor A. R. Hatton, of Northwestern University, in giving to the country, over the radio, the program on constructive economy of a committee of the National Municipal League, is comparable to that of the Chinese official who approved of the corruption of courts in his community because it discouraged litigation. It is the same process of ratiocination as of that other Chinese, in Lamb's *Essay on Roast Pig*, who burned the house to cook the pig. The absurdity of this viewpoint should be especially evident at this time when those who have heretofore been strident in their insistence that there shall be less government in business are now demanding (as the barnyard fowls sought Chantecler when the hawks threatened) that government shall come to their rescue and perform services never before contemplated and assumed with the greatest reluctance, under pressure of necessity, by conscientious public administrators.

Still another obstruction to good government movements is that resulting from "best citizens" who, for reasons of gain, intense partisanship, or desire for office of an important character, lend their names and influence to retard the onward march of their community. You cannot have burglars without a "fence," and local gangs cannot persist without "best citizens" to finance their campaigns and give them respectable sanction. These "best citizens," because they have education, position, and sufficient means (all of which should deter them from their unholy alliances), are more rightly subject to commination than the bosses, many of whom grew up in squalor, without advantages of schooling or home, and in the lowest surroundings. Of the two, the latter are the more respectable.

This is a depressing picture, no doubt, but the first duty of the combatant is to know what he must fight. Let the citizen, therefore, who loves his community and his country be made aware of and eradicate before it is too late the voracious political termites which otherwise, unnoticed and undisturbed, will eat away the beams and pillars of the house of government until it suddenly crumbles and falls. "Justice and truth are a thousand men," sings Judas Maccabaeus in Handel's great oratorio, but they are not counted that way in the election returns. The young son of Macduff, told by his mother that all who swear and lie are traitors and must be hanged, replies that the swearers and liars are fools if they permit that, "for there are liars and swearers enow to beat the honest men and hang up them." Goodness will not gush forth as water from the rock when Moses struck it; nor will privilege collapse like the walls of Jericho at the blast of a trumpet. The seeker for good government indubitably has the odds against him, and heavy odds. All the more, then, let him gird on his armor, raise his oriflamme, and advance.

LECTURE IV

Helps

THERE IS a right and a wrong way to perform the simplest acts, and the consequences of one or the other may be extremely far-reaching. To drop medicine from a bottle, the thumb should be placed under the bottle to control and support it. The label should be held up, not on the lower side of the bottle, otherwise the prescription may become moist and illegible. How obvious it ought to be, then, that if there is a preferable method of doing ordinary things like these, the best technique should be utilized in the most important business of the republic, the business of government. In a democracy, nevertheless, the office boy who diligently polishes up the handle of the big front door of an attorney's firm may become the ruler of the Queen's navy, and a Member of Parliament be elected because he can crow like a cock, or at Conservative bazaars shoot cigarettes or playing cards held by his wife in her teeth. Plato could see the folly of selecting incompetent men as public officials, but perceived nothing absurd in the election of admirals and generals. We reverse this process, and expect men whose life's work has been in totally dissimilar fields to spring like Athene from the brow of Zeus fully armed, and

instantly to become, for a short term, successful municipal and county administrators. To suggest that one's
family physician should be elected by popular vote because of his views on cancellation of foreign debts would
seem to everyone ridiculous, but it is no more absurd
than asking middle-aged or older men of affairs, wholly
inexperienced in municipal administration and burdened
with political obligations, suddenly and without preparation to take on a new profession and administer the
complex affairs of the modern municipal entity. We are
like the boy who, after reading Blackstone for half an
hour, remarked in disgust that he was sorry to have
learned the law.

There is, however, a dawning realization in our country
that local government is a great business enterprise, that
the city is not merely a political subdivision, but a business corporation, and that to conduct it successfully
requires professional skill. There has been an extraordinary development of sound technique in municipal
administration during the last twenty-five years. If purpose to secure and hold good local execution of public
affairs had kept pace with improved methods, we should
now be having in our several communities the right kind
of city and county government.

While three groups (the municipal analysts, the plan-
ners, and the managers) are exerting a pronounced and
increasing influence on local government, administration
by experts in a democracy needs leavening. Professional people are sometimes notional and cranky: *"il y a
fagots et fagots,* which, translated freely, means: "An
expert may be a stick." They often reach the conclusion

they think is desired by their employers, and very few are on the public's side in utility matters. They believe, with La Fontaine, that "the opinion of the strongest is always best," and at times deserve the cynical, nonprofessional definition of an expert as "a person who is a long way from home." Again, the scientific administrator must not get too far ahead of his government and the ordinary man. It is not so silly as it seems that the office boy to an attorney's firm becomes ruler of the navy: he represents the average viewpoint, and acts as a Sancho Panza to prevent tilting at windmills. The nonprofessional mayor and council are as important for the proper working of the city-manager plan as the manager himself. The public usually, and managers themselves occasionally, have not recognized that fact.

Having in mind these encouragements and others that might be adduced, can it not fairly be said that notwithstanding all the obstacles and hindrances to efficient local government, the chances of success are not hopeless, and that difficulties merely offer the greater challenge? The example of good government is contagious. Cleveland's adoption in 1924 of the city-manager plan helped Cincinnati to obtain it. Cincinnati's success inspired its neighbor, Hamilton, Ohio, a city of 50,000, to emulate its example with a closely similar form. Hamilton was formerly one of the worst boss-ridden cities in the country, but for several years it has been extremely well governed. The oft-quoted aphorism "People get the kind of government they deserve" is not entirely true. Two hundred and thirty-two thousand people spelled with pencil, in the last farcical mayoralty election in

New York City, the name of McKee, who had in a short
term achieved truly remarkable results, and many thousands more would have written in his name had pencils
been furnished by the election officials. There are many
cities in the land which are corrupt, but not contented.

As William James said in *The Moral Equivalent of
War*:

> *Why should they (citizens) not blush with indig-
> nant shame if the community that owns them is
> vile in any way whatsoever? Individuals, daily more
> numerous, now feel this civic passion. It is only a
> question of blowing on the spark till the whole
> population gets incandescent, and on the ruins of
> the old morals of military honor, a stable system of
> morals of civic honor builds itself up. What the
> whole community comes to believe in grasps the
> individual as in a vise. The war function has
> grasped us so far; but constructive interests may
> some day seem so less imperative and impose on
> the individual a hardly lighter burden.*

LECTURE V

Changing Views—The Remedy

WITH MORE general recognition of the importance of
city and county in the governmental scheme, there has
eventuated an altered viewpoint respecting them. No
branch of the law is more interesting and in a greater

state of flux than that relating to municipal corporations. An excellent book on the subject written, say, twenty years ago is today practically obsolete because of vital changes and new problems in the interim. While it is now authoritatively settled that there is in the United States no inherent right of local self-government, many constitutions, including the Constitution of Ohio in 1912, have been amended so as to give cities home rule. Statutes have been passed allowing cities to adopt all kinds of charters, and even in some instances, within limitations, to fix their own tax rates. But the right of home rule has been kept within definite limits, and the fields of finance, policing, health, sanitation, taxation, and local courts are still reserved for exclusive state action.

The grant of home rule has been a boon to the cities; it should be equally helpful to counties that may succeed in obtaining it.

If the hopes of those who believe in democracy are to be measurably realized and the characterization by Bryce, a generation ago, of the government of cities as "the one conspicuous failure of the United States" is to be obliterated, we must have better education, a new code of morals, new social standards, and leadership in city and county affairs.

Civic education must begin with the youngest and extend through high schools and colleges. It must diffuse the truth that local government is not, as now considered by many, the least important branch of government, but the most vital. For such it surely is. The national government, in time of peace, touches the citizen but casually, indirectly, and slightly. Local government, how-ever, affects him and those dear to him constantly, im-mediately, and weightily; it concerns his life, safety, and happiness. It is of far greater financial importance to him than state or national government. State government in Ohio in 1931 cost $79,000,000. In the same period, Ohio cities and counties spent three and a half times as much. But more important than financial considerations, the citizen judges the national government, with which he is only slightly familiar, by that government with which he is in daily contact. If he has no respect for his city and county governments and considers them undependable, corrupt, and undeserving of loyalty, his appraisal of the national government will be similar, and his resolution to support it in time of need will be weakened.

So there must be discarded the prevalent opinion that city government and county government are the lowest branches of administration, and that the holding of state and national office constitutes advancement. There is no higher peacetime activity than creating and per-petuating good local government.

The youth of the country must be familiarized with the great names and achievements in civic endeavor, as they are now taught the names and records of the na-tion's warriors and statesmen. How many have even heard of Folk in St. Louis, Clarke in Minneapolis, Kent and Fisher in Chicago, Heney in San Francisco, Jerome and Mitchell in New York, Pendleton and Hunt in Cincinnati, Tom Johnson in Cleveland, and Whitlock and Jones in Toledo? Young men and women must be made to realize that these civic knights displayed as fine a heroism as the most valiant soldiers on the field of

honor. These latter risked their lives out of love for
country, but they fought for a united people and against
a known foe in their wager of battle. The civic warrior
must needs possess moral bravery as well. His motives
will be misunderstood and misinterpreted. His good
name may be filched. He may be subjected to ridicule
and calumny without possibility of reply. Instead of
being one of a great army, all united and acclaimed,
scoffed at he holds the pass or the bridge with few or
alone. He must face corruption and danger as Banquo
did the witches:

> *Speak then to me, who neither beg nor fear*
> *Your favours nor your hate.*

Surely it is a lame and faulty education that overlooks
such effort or treats it as petty and undeserving of
attention. Textbooks must include chapters on what has
been done, is being done, and can be done in the cities of
this urban country. Boy- and girl-scout manuals must be
enlarged to include in the list of good turns daily devotion
to the affairs of one's community. More young men and
women must be taught the oath of the Athenian youth,
which was as follows:

> *We will never bring disgrace to this, our city, by*
> *any act of dishonesty or cowardice, nor ever desert*
> *our suffering comrades in the ranks; we will fight*
> *for the ideals and sacred things of the city, both*
> *alone and with many; we will revere and obey the*
> *city's laws and do our best to incite a like respect*
> *and reverence in those above us who are prone to*
> *annul or to set them at naught; we will strive un-*

*ceasingly to quicken the public's sense of civic duty;
thus, in all these ways, we will transmit this city not
only no less, but greater, better, and more beautiful than it was transmitted to us;*

and the words of Pericles: "We differ from other states
in regarding the man who holds aloof from public life,
not as quiet, but as useless."

With better education, civil and religious, influential
persons will no longer be pinchbeck benefactors of their
community. New social standards will compel them to
adhere, as in England, to principles of absolute honesty
in public affairs.

An educated and morally aroused electorate is indispensable for the success of democracy. But leaders are
likewise essential. It is the duty of those who have had
the best educational advantages to become such leaders
for civic, as well as national, righteousness. The struggle
for civic ideals put into practical operation is worthy of
the greatest devotion and self-sacrifice. Let none hang
back to ask: "Am I worthy or capable of so large a task?"
Let him inquire: "What can I do to help?" Let youth
consecrate itself before the altar of this noble cause, for
"As the judge of the people is himself so are his officers,
and what manner of man the ruler of the city is, such are
all they that dwell therein."

23

First International Congress of

Comparative Law

(OCTOBER 25, 1932)

Mr Seasongood's talk to the Cincinnati Bar Association is here reprinted from the Ohio Law Reporter, *Vol. 37 (Dec. 19, 1932), p. 306. His discourse on the 1937 Second International Congress is printed in the* Law Library Journal, *Vol. 31, No. 2 (Mar. 1938), p. 47. Substantial portions of both addresses appear in his talk before the Travel Club of Cincinnati, printed in the* Enquirer, *Section 4 (Mar. 27, 1938).*

IN 1924, having attended the meeting of the American Bar in London, I wrote, for the *American Bar Association Journal*, Vol. x, No. 9 (Sept. 1924), p. 667, the log of the *Laconia*, the *Pinta* (free translation, "half pint") of the lawyers' fleet. As the Statute of Limitations has presumably run against that indiscretion, I now, as one of the delegates of our Cincinnati Bar Association, commit another, as follows:

The First International Congress of Comparative Law convened Monday morning, August 2, 1932, in the Hall of Knights of the Parliament Buildings at The Hague.

This hall is a large, simple, three-century-old assembly place with a very high wooden ceiling, the walls hung partway up with oriental rugs and studded above with small stained-glass windows exhibiting the arms of different Dutch cities. If this Congress had been held twenty years ago, the Chamber would have been filled with luxuriant, flowing beards, mustaches, side whiskers, and star-y-pointing pompadours. At this reunion in 1932, aside from one old gentleman who looked exactly like the pictures of George B. Shaw and the vari-colored, drooping mustachios of Sir William Holdsworth as flowing as those of the terra-cotta sea lion in the courtyard of the Peace Palace, most of the delegates were indistinguishable, both in appearance and dress, from our own nationals. At a session of the World Court held later, which all were privileged to attend, the same thing was noticeable in the magnificent-looking jurists comprising that Court, fifteen of whom were seated on the bench when their opinion was delivered in French by Adatli, their Japanese presiding officer. If one were not told from which country a judge came, one could not divine, by looking at him, of which nation he was the representative. Verily, the safety razor has changed the face of man.

The address of welcome (*discours*) was excellent and briefly made by Jonkheer F. Beelaerts van Blokland, Dutch Minister of Foreign Affairs, in perfect and readily understandable French. But one of the inevitable great difficulties of world congresses is the confusion of tongues. Even if you adopt one language as official, it, when spoken by learned gentlemen from various quarters of the world, often takes on the character of many languages, so that the differences between *langue d'oc* and *langue d'oïl* are slight in comparison.

Certainly the French of certain of the learned gentlemen was not what one hears at the Comédie Française. For many of the brethren, the proceedings were similar to the report by Casca, in Julius Caesar, referring to Cicero speaking in Greek: "But, for my part, it was Greek to me." But, differing from Casca's account that those who understood Cicero's Greek smiled and shook their heads, this procedure was followed as well by those who did not comprehend the French of Professor I. de Koschembahr-Lyskowski or of Professor Freiherr Claudius von Schwerin.

Lord Shaftesbury, when chancellor, caused the head of a special pleader to be poked through a prolix bill in equity he had drafted and required him to wear his redundant and verbose collar of shame. In like manner, an excellent idea in all international and other gatherings would be, if a warning were served on speakers who bow the head and talk confidentially into notes, that the huissier, usher, sergeant-at-arms, bailiff, or what you will, would come up behind and give what wrestlers call the "rabbit punch."

To those having a fair knowledge of French, the efforts of many of the learned brethren were an encouragement to try oneself and recall the violin teacher of George III, mentioned in one of Lowell's essays, who classified violinists as good, bad, and those who could not play at all, and congratulated His Majesty on having already advanced to the second class.

There followed an "allocution" by Professor A. S. d'Bustamente, former president and now judge of the Permanent Court of International Justice, and president of the International Academy of Comparative Law, under whose auspices the Congress was held, and a lengthy "arousement" by Professor Balogh, secretary of the Congress.

Just what the difference is between a *discours* and an *allocution* I am not able to say, although during the week of the Congress there were plenty of both.

The program referred to the opening meeting of the Congress as a *séance solennelle d'ouverture*. The managers were determined it should be such. When Professor Wigmore made a delightful, brief address, speaking without notes and, endeavoring to inject a little humor into a long and heavy session, opined whether you read Quintilian or Dickens or Balzac or look at Daumier's works, the legal profession is the same everywhere, and (by way of pleasantry) lawyers everywhere curse the court, and judges in all countries lament the dullness and ignorance of the bar, you could feel the assembly listening with bated breath, an international shudder shook the rugs on the walls, and the Master of the Rolls solemnly and very pronouncedly moved his head in denial. Mr. Wigmore stated that the Academy had worked for two years to have this Congress, which was intended to harmonize legal thought of more than fifty countries. Recalling three ephemeral efforts toward this end over a period of forty years . . . he urged that the present Congress should not adjourn without arranging for permanent, periodical meetings. He also suggested that there ought to be a world organization of the entire legal profession—judges, professors, notaries public, publicists, police and advocates—asserting that we are the only profession in the world having none. Seven hundred international associations are listed at Geneva, from beekeepers to veterinarians and zoologists, but the legal profession is not included in their number.

My contribution to the Congress was an insistence that one of the printed programs should be cut up and pasted on the bulletin board, so that an approximation of what was going on in the different sections could be had; also, a resolution in favor of Legal Aid for the Poor, which was referred to the Academy.

In the evening of this full day, at twenty-one and a half o'clock (the European way of saying half past nine), there began the first of an elaborate series of receptions. This was held in the Hall of Knights and was offered to the Congress by the Government of the Netherlands, headed by the Secretary of Foreign Affairs and his agreeable wife. Hospitality rivaled that of the Bar Association meeting in London in 1924. It was very interesting and pleasant to be bumping into legal personages from all countries of Europe and even from South America, China, Egypt, Turkey, South Africa, and the Philippines. The invitations called for evening dress and decorations. Three thrones for the Royal Family were placed on the dais where the speakers and officials had assembled in the morning, and the hall, brilliantly lighted and with the diplomatic corps and numerous attendants in uniforms, presented a festive appearance. The Dutch official contour lends itself to decorations, and most of the adornments appeared to be so large and glittering that the iridescent starbursts of fireworks in our honor at one of the later receptions at Scheveningen seemed pallid in comparison. The Minister from the United States was dedight with but a single decoration in the locality of the fifth rib where Joab surreptitiously stuck his sword into his brother Amasa, and our American naval attaché at The Hague modestly wore two small ones. A globular high personage of the Dutch government was as studded with glittering baubles as the Hindenburg statue in Berlin is with nails or a baked ham is with cloves, the only free places on his torso being where a large red sash embellished his shirt diagonally and the presumably vacant space beneath a spreading patriarchal white beard.

If there is any scarcity of food and drink in the world, it must be in part because so much was assembled and consumed at these various receptions. The principal engrosser was a Japanese reputed to be a delegate, but I firmly believe a wrestler in disguise. Some of these jujitsu professionals weigh in the neighborhood of 300 pounds, and having seen this one in gustatory action, it is remarkable to me how they keep their weight so low. He dug himself in at one of the long buffet tables as if he were in the trenches around Mukden, sat down at the festal board, and surrounded himself with food and champagne, which he continued to macerate and imbibe through most of the evening, leaving others to engage in the unworthy art of conversation. My fellow delegate from the Cincinnati Bar Association had been an end on the Harvard football team. This training stood him in good stead. He made a brilliant run around the Japanese and a flying tackle for some champagne, with very successful results for his party.

There were numerous women lawyers at the convention. Pierre LePaulle, of Paris, a brilliant graduate of the Harvard Law School, and his wife are both *avocats* practicing together. She says there are some 200 women lawyers in Paris. There was a pulchritudinous woman professor of law of the University of Milan, and one in professorial robes on the faculty of Law of the University of Leyden, when we visited there. One of the ladies, Miss Mitchell, also of Paris, has written a book on the French Law of Checks which is regarded as an authority, and there were numerous others who, at receptions, engaged in the frivolous pastime of dancing to American jazz, with apparent enjoyment. Checks in French law are money, there is no stopping them, and the signer is the loser in case of forgery.

At four o'clock in the afternoon the World Court announced the decision before referred to. The proceedings were simple. Court was opened promptly with even less formality than in the Supreme Court at Washington. Our representative, Kellogg, was not present. The judges wore black robes with white lace bands or bibs (although that is probably not the correct word for so great a tribunal). The opinion took about three quarters of an hour to deliver. Time is doubtless not a matter of importance with the court; but one wonders, in view of copies of the opinion being delivered simultaneously in French and English to all interested parties, why a summary or statement of the conclusion would not have been enough. The proceedings of the court are both in French and English. Many colleagues from the United States who attended in the large room where the court sat felt regret at the niggardly, and to me, unreasonable attitude of our country in not contributing the expenses of the judge who represents the United States.

Friday afternoon there were exercises incident to the unveiling of a statue to Louis Renault at the Peace Palace. After one of the brethren had listened for more than an hour and a half to overfervid addresses in French, and hastened for refreshment to the cup of tea which was served each afternoon, he exclaimed: "Why do they make all that fuss of that Renault, when the Rolls Royce is just as good?"

The French eulogistic memorial style of oratory appeared to a Swedish friend, from the University of Lund, too personal, too dramatic, and too sentimental. "What," he said, "would these orators with the quaver in their voices reminiscent of the old-fashioned melodrama have said of Grotius or someone else of the very first rank in International Law?" Perhaps we have become imbued with feelings similar to those of the crusty English judge who said that "eloquence reminded him of nothing so much as moldy wedding cake," and who, after reading *Romeo and Juliet*, threw it aside in disgust "as a mere tissue of improbabilities." But, in listening, one thought with appreciation of the elder Holmes's delightful *My Hunt After the Captain*, in contrasting the Anglo-American more reserved style of expression. Still, the oratory was easy and beautiful, and the voices sonorous and musical, like Alexandrines of Corneille or Racine declaimed by Bernhardt or Sully.

The proceedings were presided over by one who had been a colleague of Renault, Professor Lyon-Caen, an extraordinary old gentleman variously reported to be eighty-nine or ninety-three years old, looking and dressed like the professor of an age that is past, and somewhat as one would imagine the ancient officer of Daudet's *Le Siège de Berlin*. The venerable teacher was vigorous, handsome, and distinguished, and went through the long proceedings, as did his fellow senex, Loder, and Mrs. Renault, the very dear, sweet-looking widow of the great man, without apparent weariness.

For the final session, the Congress reverted to the Hall of Knights. It listened to telegraphic responses from the Queen of Holland and Queen Mother to the salutations that had been addressed to them. The allocution of M. Piola Casselli, president of the Chamber at the Court of Cassation of Rome . . . referred to the Italian conference with France for uniform law and Italy's own attempt at uniform law. (The Scandinavian countries have made good progress with a similar effort.) He emphasized the importance of international fraternization among lawyers, and, in order that Mussolini might not be forgotten, referred to this as being the tenth year of the Fascist government.

Our own James Brown Scott, secretary of the Carnegie Endowment for International Peace, and attached to the Permanent Court of International Justice, advanced in perfect French the proposition that international law should be the law of the United States, and urged the setting up of an international body to determine if state or national United States law is consistent with international law. After Professor Ernst Heymann, of Berlin, secretary of the Prussian Academy of Learning, had vehemently asserted in an address made in both German and French that it is a sacred duty to unite law and make it uniform, reports from the various sections were proffered.

Professor Edouard Lambert, of the University of Lyons, a most emphatic, clear, and eloquent speaker, referred to himself as having been the general housemaid for his section, pounded the desk and shouted in the enthusiasm with which he summarized the reports for the general section: the suggestion that there should be an international organization for the documentation of international papers had been considered by the section, but there was no organization that could do this and there appeared to be no machinery for setting up one. Future meetings of the Congress must be devoted to study of history of all law with fewer suggestions and shorter discussions. In an inspirational close, he pleaded that as Bologna was formerly the center for the teaching of law, so there should be a new Bologna, that is, a university with a faculty expressly for the teaching of comparative law.

The official closing address of the session was spoken (almost chanted) without notes by M. Henri Levy-Ullmann, professor of law at the University of Paris, vice-president of the Academy of International Comparative Law, under whose auspices the Congress was held. Here was French oratory at its best, interspersed with poetry and appropriate quotations, never wanting for a word and with a beautiful clarity and orderly arrangement worthy of Descartes.

In the afternoon the company motored to Delft, only a short distance. There, in the old (called New) Gothic Church, in which the organist played appropriate airs as we entered, James B. Scott spoke briefly in French and laid a wreath at the tomb of Grotius. Thence we proceeded to the University of Leyden where delightful ceremonies were had in the Convocation Hall. The head of the university, in black plush cap and gown, ascended a

high pulpit and addressed the company in Latin. If given
a little goatee, he would have been a Van Dyke to the
life. Some of the brethren who did not know "sap" from
"sapiens" and who, when they meet a graduate of their
college, say: "I am an alma mater of that institution myself," and applaud vociferously at commencement when
the Latin orator bows to the ladies and refers to them as
filiae pulcherrimae, again took on the same appearance
of understanding as they did when gentlemen from Lat-
via spoke French.

The staircase leading to the faculty room was reminiscent of that part of the Dutch school of painting represented by Jan Steen, being decorated with charcoal draw-
ings on the wall by former students seeming to have had
more aptitude for art than law or divinity. But of the
portraits in the faculty room itself Professor Wigmore,
quoting Lord McMillan (a keen and charming law lord
of the English Court of Appeal), asserted that more
great men were represented by the pictures in that room
than in any other similar place in Europe, and Lord
McMillan himself referred to a great Scotch scholar who,
when banished, took refuge at Leyden because he considered it the most scholarly place in Europe.

The tea that followed at the art museum in Leyden
was a somewhat riotous affair, the polite wishing to hear
the courteous address of welcome by the Burgomaster in
one room, while others, feeling they had already heard
enough welcomings for the rest of their lives, and led by
the Japanese wrestler, made a hasty attack on the food
and drink in the adjoining room, with so great a resulting
hubbub that the hospitable words were lost in the clatter

of dishes and the cacophony of loud conversation and tea guzzling. Finally, someone pulled the folding doors shut, and when they were reopened, the Japanese wrestler, abetted by sundry poor imitators, had again performed prodigious feats of mastication, so that only a few crumbs and dregs were left for those who had listened.

Most of the delegates in attendance now dispersed. But for those who remained over Sunday, there was an instructive trip to the Island of Wieringen whence the causeway diking the Zuider Zee had been recently completed to Friesland. The dream fifty years ago of one of those crazy enthusiasts who make progress in the world possible had been realized, although all the wise men had prophesied that the project was impossible for military, financial, and engineering reasons.

The first Congress was a step in the direction of international amity, just as had been the 1924 visit of the American Bar Association to London. Before that time many of our brethren accepted, as their idea of the English, what they had learned in their school-day American histories and had seen in the comic papers and the stage. None, however, who visited the Inns of Court, Westminster Hall, and who enjoyed commensality at the Guild Hall and elsewhere will continue to have feelings of dislike and distrust. So, at this assembly at The Hague, in the traditional land of religious freedom and scholarship, the land of Grotius and Spinoza, the greatest benefit was not the start toward unifying the law of different countries. It was rather the inspiration from seeing in the flesh and assembling with many great figures in our profession, of many lands, and realizing from the spoken word and the hearty handclasps that however far away and diverse their customs, all are brethren in seeking to establish a more perfect justice and understanding among the nations.

➤➤➤-➤➤➤-➤➤➤-➤➤➤-➤➤➤-➤➤《《《-《《《-《《《-《《《-《《《-《《《

24

New Methods in City Government

(FEBRUARY 9, 1933)

*In this address to the New York Economic Club,
Mr. Seasongood gave an over-all picture of the move-
ment to reform the Cincinnati city government. For
writings dealing with this theme see his "The Tri-
umph of Good Government in Cincinnati" in the
Annals of the American Academy of Political and
Social Science, Vol. 199 (Sept. 1938), p. 83; also
"New Methods in City Government," in The Con-
sensus, the official organ of the National Economic
League, Vol. XVII, No. 4 (Apr. 1933), p. 4*

IN 1904 Lincoln Steffens referred to Cincinnati as "corrupt and contented" and termed it the worst governed
city in the United States. He denounced the Cincinnati
and Hamilton County Republican machine and urged
the voters to cast their ballot for the Republican state
ticket, but against the local Republican county candidates. In 1906 and again in 1908 legislative investigating
committees showed, before they were stopped by hostile
courts, a most depraved condition of public affairs in Cincinnati and Hamilton County. The disclosures in these
investigations were very similar to those of the recent
Hofstadter Committee. Nevertheless, the rule of the
bosses, Cox and Hynicka, continued for more than
twenty years. The city was grossly misgoverned, and

the citizens appeared to have lapsed into an attitude of cynicism, indifference, and despair.

In the last couple of years, however, professors of political science in the universities of Chicago and Michigan, and other authorities, have referred to Cincinnati either as one of the two best governed cities in the United States or as the best governed large city anywhere.

The forces of good government have prevailed in five successive elections, and by January 1, 1934, good government will have been continuous for eight years. In that time, before the depression period, the whole physical appearance of the city was changed. New streets, boulevards, viaducts, parks, sewers, and other extensive municipal improvements were made. Expenditures for recreation, health, welfare, planning, and every useful purpose were enormously increased, and many great private undertakings requiring city co-operation have been completed. Nevertheless, inheriting $7,400,000 of deficiency bonds and a heavy general bonded indebtedness, the city has paid off more than $6,000,000 of such deficiency bonds, and its net non-self-supporting debt has not been increased but has been reduced over $2½,000,000 since January 1, 1926.

The savings to its citizens, therefore, have run into the millions directly and indirectly: $1,500,000 a year saved in gas and electric franchises; $650,000 in one street; $263,000 saving in one year on the same amount of street materials used in 1925; in three years $80,000 in street repairs with seven per cent increase in wages; $500,000 in acquisition of an airport of almost 1,000 acres; and huge amounts not susceptible of exact calculation, resulting from better and cleaner streets, improved morale of city employees, reduced fire losses, and diminution in crime.

In accomplishing these results, Cincinnati has utilized labor-saving devices and experts in the field of government, as well as the patriotic effort of its own citizenship.

What are the causes of Cincinnati's extraordinary transformation?

First: its amended charter providing for it a new form of government.

Second: widespread citizen interest and the ability to enlist in the city's service many of those capable and desirous of rendering sound aid in an unselfish manner. Women, particularly, in Cincinnati have helped in an organized way doing, without compensation, election chores ordinarily performed, as their livelihood, by boss-driven ward and precinct executives.

Third: the government of Cincinnati is based on equality for all, absence of politician intermediaries, and the deracination of privilege.

Finally: a genuine Merit System is in force, with the whole body of municipal employees independent of political favor, taken out of partisan politics and prohibited from making contributions to political campaigns.

What has been accomplished in Cincinnati can be effectuated with equal resolution and leadership in New York and other large cities of the country. The attainment of good city government in New York, it must be admitted, is more difficult, but it is not impossible. Supposed insuperable objections inhering in the country's greatest city, such as the large foreign element, the far-reaching power of the dominant machine, shifting population and numerous persons of the better type living outside of the city, offer difficulties, it is true. But every city has some of these handicaps and each city has its own special obstacles to overcome, some of which are not present in New York; and New York has certain advantages such as its large number of powerful persons of the best ability. These should compensate and fairly balance the disadvantages referred to.

It will be the greatest pity if the present period of widespread distress does not result in eventual good through improved local government, which will benefit not only the cities concerned, but eventually the politics and welfare of the entire country.

>>>->>>->>>->>>->>>->>>>((<-(((-(((-(((-(((-(((

25

Union League Club of Chicago

(FEBRUARY 9, 1934)

Mr. Seasongood's address appeared in Men and
Events, *the printed bulletin of the club, under the
title "Citizens in Action," Mar. 1934. See the speaker's "Cincinnati and Home Rule," in* Ohio State
Law Journal, *Vol. 9, No. 1 (Winter 1948), p. 98.
On one occasion he debated with Mayor Hoan of
Milwaukee before the Chicago Public Forum about
which was the best governed city. Chicago was not
a contender.*

I HOPE you will not think what is said with respect to
Cincinnati is said in any boastful spirit, but rather as an
indication of what can be accomplished and should be
accomplished. I do not want to be like the Los Angeles
person who, when someone said: "I understand you
have 365 days of sunshine a year in your city," replied:
"That is a very conservative statement."

But these are the facts with respect to Cincinnati. It
has the lowest tax rate of any city of over 300,000 population. Formerly it had, in addition to its ordinary sources
of taxation, an occupational tax, which has been repealed.
The bonded debt of the city has been reduced some
$3,000,000 from the net bonded indebtedness as it ex-
isted on January 1, 1926, when the new order went in.

This, despite the fact that many great improvements have been made.

What has been accomplished in Cincinnati has been done with extraordinary success also in Hamilton County. Our county treasurer is the tax collector, not merely a tax receiver. Our percentage of delinquency in taxes is far the lowest of any county in Ohio, and I suppose anywhere. Our delinquency now is something like twelve per cent. The reform treasurers have collected about a million and a quarter in taxes delinquent from former administrations. This amount was collected with an expenditure of $2,400 for the salary of a young lawyer who was just out of law school. The treasurer's office operates with a minimum of personnel employed. There are either fourteen or eighteen in the whole office who collect all the taxes for the county, the schools, and the city. Our sister city, Cleveland, which collects about twice as much in taxes, has about four or five times as many employees in the treasurer's office. Our collection expense is a quarter of one per cent.

We have no fixers, no political lawyers, or anybody to get your valuations reduced. Our auditor made a valuation invoking for his assistance the departments of the University of Cincinnati for buildings on a definite basis of depreciation and standards for valuation, and of the real-estate board on land values.

We closed the past year with a real money balance of $900,000. At the end of the year, instead of that being merely lost, it is used as a basis for restoring salaries of the lowest paid city employees who were cut on a graded scale beginning at five per cent on the first thousand and running up to twenty per cent in the high brackets.

The five per cent cut was just about twice as much as the "voluntary" campaign assessment the city employees used to pay. It was so voluntary that if you did not pay it you were out on the street the next day.

The indirect benefits of a good government are very widespread. Our fire losses, for instance, have been tremendously reduced. Why? First, because our streets, instead of being as they formerly were like the European battlefield—pitted with holes—are now perfectly smooth and level. The fire department can now make a run and get there a few minutes sooner, and that means the difference between a serious fire and taking hold of this catastrophe at the earliest possible moment. Our fire losses were only $750,000 last year, which was extraordinarily low. Another reason is the improved morale of the fire department. Formerly people got into the fire department quite openly at the solicitation of local politicians. Men got in or got promoted and their loyalty was to the man who got them in or who made their promotion effective rather than to the department. Now they all know that there is a complete merit system. They all take the examinations for promotion. They know that it is on the level, that anybody can compete and anybody can take the examination, and their efficiency is very greatly increased. In a city like Kansas City, which operates under a political system, although having a good council manager charter, too, but where the selection is made without any shame or concealment on the basis of political adherence and at the request of political leaders, the fire losses were approximately twice as great.

Moreover, we have had a decrease of major crime in the region of Cincinnati, which I again attribute to the improved morale of the police department. Under the former administrations, seventy of our policemen were sent to Leavenworth for complicity in bootlegging and they were sent on the state's evidence of one of the councilmen who confessed to having bribed them. You can see how that undermines the morale of the police force. Under this system again, a policeman has no one who will favor him. If he gets in trouble, no one is going to help him out. He is expected to do his duty and he will get along all right, and if he merits promotion he has a chance to obtain it. The influence of any particular person helps him not at all. The result is that the police have been greatly improved likewise, and we have no racketeering whatsoever in the city of Cincinnati. I think those two are results of a government of citizens freed from political interference. You do not need anything more to show the connection between the two than the recent disclosures of the horrible prison conditions in New York City and what went on there. The relationship between the local gangsters and the political gangsters has always been close and they are also interdependent, and it is by getting away from these and curtailing their powers that you make racketeering and major crime considerably less.

Another interesting thing that we have done is in the matter of garbage and ash collection. That was formerly let to a private contracting firm. The income-tax figures published showed their income on that contract, after charging liberally for the depreciation and salaries and ordinary expenditures, of something over $100,000. The manager of that garbage company was one of the ward leaders of the Republican machine. The contract was not observed. They had stinking wagons with the lids open.

It resulted in a blighted area where the reduction was done because the smells were so bad and the whole thing was so illy attended to. Now we have motorized trailer service. I honestly believe that our health has been better because of this sanitary method. The number of flies has been lessened considerably in summer. The saving in cost also is something like $150,000 a year.

In the Water Works Department changes have been made after a study by the Bureau of Governmental Research which meant a saving of $300,000 a year and a lower water rate.

We have co-operation between the city, and the county, and the schools. These entities have formed a joint bond issuing group. They establish a tentative program of about five years. They estimate what bonds should be issued by vote of the people and what will be the effect on the tax rate. Then literature is distributed with the water bills showing the need for these bonds and what the effect will be on the tax rate as a result of them. This bond issuing group co-ordinates the bonds, and you have this extraordinary result, that whereas, formerly, bond issues were voted down in almost every instance, since the inception of this group, until this year, every bond issue that was submitted, totalling more than $30,-000,000 over a period of years, was voted on favorably by the electors.

Another instance of the fascinating nature of the opportunities for improvement in this field is a combined group of purchasing agents of these three units with the addition of our municipal university. The Laura Spelman Rockefeller Memorial Fund contributed $25,000 for perfecting it. These purchasing agents establish a standard specification for articles that are needed by all four of the purchasing agencies. In the matter of coal, for example, they found that by adopting a standard specification for coal in taking the bids for all of the units at the same time they saved, in one year, $100,000. This thing can be carried far. They have made only a beginning.

In the end the whole thing comes to this: you have to have a better social standard maintained by your persons of importance, by your universities, by your important businessmen, and by your schools, who will bring about a situation (I suppose it is all right to refer now to England in Chicago) as in England, where it is incredible that a man in public life could be guilty of dishonesty or condone or submit to it. The suggestion that you have to have local gangs because they are the tap root of the national political parties is all nonsense. England shows it is nonsense, because they have had the party system in England longer than we have in this country.

What we need is an aroused conscience and an aroused sense of responsibility toward local government. The cities must no longer be made the playthings of the national parties. It will be ruination for the national parties if they are allowed to be such. The cities and the counties must come into the place which is rightfully theirs, and it can be done if you have a determined citizenship intent upon bringing about better conditions in the locality in which they live.

➤➤➤-➤➤➤-➤➤➤-➤➤➤-➤➤➤-➤➤◄◄◄-◄◄◄-◄◄◄-◄◄◄-◄◄◄-◄◄◄

26

Forty Years of Progress in Municipal Affairs

(NOVEMBER 26–7, 1934)

*Murray Seasongood delivered this report at the
fortieth annual meeting of the National Municipal
League at Pittsburgh, Pa. It is reprinted from the
National Municipal Review, Vol. 23, No. 12 (Dec.
1934), p. 644. At the League's National Conference
on Government in Cincinnati, Nov. 27, 1951, he received its "Good Citizen" award. In May 1955 the
League named the library in its building (47 E. 68th
St., New York, N.Y.) the Murray Seasongood Library, "in recognition of his great contributions to
the improvement of local government and of his
long and constructive service to the League."*

I COME like Charles I, to talk after my head is off, although, be reassured, not like him for seven days. I am a
firm believer in rotation in office and think the policy of
our League—not more than three terms of a year each
for the president—is an excellent one. I am most happy,
also, in the choice of my successor as president, Dr.
Harold W. Dodds, President of Princeton University.
That he is willing to serve as our chief officer, notwithstanding his heavy duties as directing head of a great university, is a matter of congratulation and encouragement
for the future of the League.

The fortieth anniversary of the founding of the National Municipal League should not go unnoticed. It was organized at a conference on good city government called in Philadelphia by a distinguished list of sponsors, including Theodore Roosevelt, Louis D. Brandeis, now Mr. Justice Brandeis of the United States Supreme Court, James C. Carter, Richard H. Dana, Charles J. Bonaparte, R. Fulton Cutting, Richard Watson Gilder, John R. Procter, Wendell P. Garrison, Abram S. Hewett, Edwin L. Godkin, and Clinton Rogers Woodruff, the last of whom is still Honorary Secretary of the National Municipal League. Great names these, and we are proud to carry on the institution they initiated. James C. Carter, of New York, became the first president of the League. He was the acknowledged leader of the bar of this country. Charles J. Bonaparte, of Baltimore, another of the signers of the original call, succeeded him as president, and the present Chief Justice of the United States, the Honorable Charles E. Hughes, also served in that capacity.

The League has been an important agency for the improvement of local government in this country. Founded at a time when municipal and county government were at perhaps the lowest stage, it has witnessed extraordinary improvement in its, for a United States reform organization, very long life. Since its birth practically all of the following have developed in local affairs in this country, and many since it attained its majority—some in the last few years: the growth of the Merit System; initiative and referendum; the short ballot; the nonpartisan ballot; the Massachusetts form of ballot; proportional representation; planning for cities, counties, states, and regions; zoning, including experiments with setbacks and excess condemnation; the right of home rule in local affairs, city and county; the commission plan, succeeded by the council-manager plan of government; bureaus of governmental research; permanent registration of voters.

It is appropriate, as I leave office, to present a brief review of what has happened during the past three years in the field of local government as well as a review of the activity of the organization itself.

First of all, the growth of the council-manager plan is encouraging. Twenty-one cities have adopted this form of government in the last three years, and reports from all of them indicate that better service is being rendered at lower cost.

Most significant of all, however, are the inroads that have been made upon that unit of local government dubbed by H. S. Gilbertson, when he was with the National Municipal League, the "dark continent of American politics"—the county. Three years ago no county in the United States was operating under what could truthfully be called the manager form of county government.

Today, however, we can look upon six counties operating successfully under the manager form of government —three in Virginia, two in California, and one in North Carolina—and can at the same time welcome a newcomer to the ranks, Douglas County, Nebraska, which includes Omaha. In Hamilton (Cincinnati), Cuyahoga (Cleveland), Lucas (Toledo), and Mahoning (Youngstown) in Ohio, at the recent election, commissions of which I am a member in our county were elected to frame county home-rule charters for submission to the electors.

. . .

Turning now to consider the affairs of the National Municipal League itself:

The League has not only weathered the peril of the depression, but has improved its financial condition during the depression period. Never before has the organization been in such a position to extend its influence. During the past three years, the crisis in municipal finance has created opportunities which have led to wider contacts for the League. More than fifty other national organizations have co-operated with us in the attempt to establish citizens' councils so as to withstand the hysterical cutting and slashing of municipal budgets and curtailment of essential services and to transfer destructive into constructive economy. Approximately 170 such councils have been organized to date.

The National Municipal League has great traditions. It should continue to be the leader in the fight to improve local government in this country. Now, again, when local government ought to attract the attention it deserves, it meets with certain serious handicaps: the overshadowing importance of the federal government with the assumption by it of services that should be local; the shortage of revenues arising from tax-limitation drives, shrinking duplicates and large delinquency in taxes and assessments. The need is greater than it has ever been to safeguard and strengthen sound local government and to acquaint the people with its importance. May our League continue valiantly to seek accomplishment of the objects for which it was founded forty years ago. May its efforts continue with success until the battle is safely won, which is another way of saying "forever."

꙾꙾꙾꙾꙾꙾꙾

27

Introducing Amelia Earhart

(MARCH 24, 1936)

Murray Seasongood made this address at a dinner given in honor of Miss Earhart by the Smith College Club. On Feb. 22, 1934, he made the Rally Day address at Smith College.

WHEN I first learned of the honor and pleasure conferred on me by the Cincinnati Smith Club in permitting me to introduce their distinguished guest speaker of tonight, I began to cast about in my mind for any special qualifications I might have for this important duty. After I have finished, you, too, will probably be indulging in a similar inquiry.

I am not an aviator, although I possess a frame that is somewhat heavier than air. I have been in the cockpit (of local politics) for more than a dozen years; so, such wings as I used to have have become frayed and warped. My controls are not good, but my power to exhaust is said to be; and whenever I have landed, I seem to have landed with a jolt, on somebody.

In general, my flights have been oratorical only. But these are often more hazardous than any other. I did make one flight in a plane while abroad about six years ago. It was not a solo flight such as the little jaunts our guest is apt to take across the Atlantic or Pacific. My wife, daughter, and three or four other passengers shared the adventure. It lasted only an hour; but, as said in Rossetti's poem *The Blessed Damozel,* "to one it seemed ten years of years." Incidentally, I gained some idea of how the Blessed Damozel felt when she "leaned out from the gold bar of Heaven." The plane shot up at least that high, and when something happened to one of the motors and the cabin filled with smoke, I thought of more poetry than I ever did or shall do in the same space of time. For instance, from *Midsummer Night's Dream,* this seemed appropriate:

> *the poet's eye, in a fine frenzy rolling*
> *doth glance from Heaven to earth, from earth to*
> *Heaven.*

Well, the plane did the rolling, and the passengers the frenzy and glancing, and all wished for "a local habitation." It was not so bad when the plane dipped on the port side, but when it came over to starboard, where I was sitting precariously, I looked down to earth, became conscious that there was no balcony or railing, and considered what a squash I should make if I got down there in too much of a hurry. I thought of Wolsey's "when he falls he falls like Lucifer, never to hope again," and preferred the more leisurely Milton *Paradise Lost* version of Lucifer's fall:

> *from morn to noon he fell from noon to dewy eve,*
> *A summer's day and with the setting sun dropped*
> *from the zenith like a falling star.*

They gave us cotton for our ears and chewing gum for our fears. Neither served the purpose. You could hear the throbbing of your temples through the cotton, and while chewing gum is a detestable habit of which I thoroughly disapprove, I found myself not reproaching my wife and daughter doing it with extreme vigor, and wishing they had given me enough to stick myself more firmly to my seat.

I spare you further details of this flight. No doubt since then, thanks to Miss Earhart and other indomitable fliers, there have been great improvements in the art of aeronautics. But these have been made without active co-operation by our immediate family. Since our adventure, we have felt toward airplaning like the late South African diamond king, Barney Barnato, toward lion hunting. When asked if he wanted to hunt lions, he replied somewhat inelegantly but with deep feeling: "I ain't lost no lion."

And now you can see why I can speak with unstinted admiration of the courage of one who flies solo, unmindful of Icarus and the Hellespont, across the Pacific from Honolulu and from Mexico City to New York and writes a book about these and her other flying expeditions, and calls it "The Fun of It." Why, she beats George Washington in firsts. He was just first in war, first in peace, and first in the hearts of his countrymen, whereas her firsts include: first woman to fly the Atlantic; first person to fly the Atlantic twice; first woman to fly an autogyro; first person to cross the United States in an autogyro; first woman to receive the Distinguished Flying Cross; first woman to receive the National Geographical Society's gold medal; first woman to make a transcontinental non-stop flight; first woman licensed in the United States to carry passengers for hire in cabin planes weighing up to

7,700 pounds; first person to solo across the Pacific from Honolulu; first person to solo from Mexico City to New York. She typifies, one might say, the American modern woman; and all the things she does, she does good-humoredly, modestly, and without losing any of her womanly charm. We shall now have the pleasure of hearing from America's intrepid aerial explorer, Miss Amelia Earhart.

-»»-»»-»»-»»-»»-»»-«««-«««-«««-«««-«««-«««-

28

Youth and the State—Clean Politics

(JULY 23, 1938)

*This address was delivered over the N.B.C. network
under the auspices of the Union of the American
Hebrew Congregations, and was printed in* Public
Opinion, *Vol. 8, No. 1 (Sept. 1938), pp. 10–11, 22.
Mr. Seasongood was a long-time member of the
Board of Governors at Hebrew Union College; a
member of the Executive Committee of the American Jewish Committee; and also the first president
of the Cincinnati chapter of that committee.*

ORDINARILY, the youth of a country are the champions of
great causes. In England, young men have, for many
years, interested themselves in politics and have aspired
to positions in the public service as a life career. But with
us this has not been so and the general attitude of young
people in this land of ours, toward the great objective of
honorable state and local politics, has not been credit-
able.

Their supineness may be illustrated by an anecdote
told of the poet James Thomson, author of *The Seasons*:
a friend found him at two o'clock in the afternoon still in
bed, and upon expressing surprise, Thomson replied:
"There is nothing to get up for."

Still, youth in these United States is not itself prima-
rily to be blamed for this dereliction. The young men and

women of our country have not been sufficiently informed, by what is taught in schools and colleges, of the vital importance, either in a financial way or in relation to national politics, of local government and of possible victories for good government they can achieve in states, counties, and cities. Likewise, they have not been roused, by their spiritual preceptors, to the moral aspects of the problems of local government.

Before the present era of unparalleled spending by the federal government and its assumption of powers previously regarded as belonging to the states, local government spent more than the sum of the expenditures of the state and national governments and still disburses vast sums. So, disregarding everything else, if it is desired to save, and to lessen the public burden of the many, any place to begin economies is where savings of large amounts may be effected. With states and cities being called on constantly to perform new and costly functions, and with the shrinkage of their available revenues for local purposes, if local government, the keystone of the arch of democracy, is to be preserved, it must be by honest, thrifty, and intelligent administration of state and local affairs.

Again, the term "local" applied to the government of subdivisions of the state is really a misnomer. Unfortunately, the government of these localities and of the states is hooked up with the national-party patronage system. The local bosses are not infrequently officers of the national-party organizations and influential in their deliberations. Many Federal officers and officials have received their training, and the prominence that made them suitable for positions on the ballot, in the domain of local politics. If they had low aims in that field, they carry them into the national field and debase it accordingly. Federal appointments are often made from recommendations of the local political organizations. So, altogether, the effect of sordid standards in the local field is felt very strongly in the national political domain.

Whenever wars have been fought, they have been waged principally by the youth of the countries concerned, often on a voluntary basis, because youth is courageous and, when aflame with what it considers a righteous cause, movingly unselfish. But the American youth do not know, except in a shadowy way, that the effort to achieve good government in one's locality is a righteous cause—indeed, the highest peacetime activity of the citizen. A book like *Twenty Years of Government in Essex County, New Jersey,* by Dr. Thomas H. Reed (New York: Appleton-Century-Crofts, Inc.; 1938), should be read. It is a thrilling narrative of how this county, in which the city of Newark is located, one of the largest and most important in the country, was wrested from a spoils organization, changed into a good government center, and preserved as such over a period of twenty years by an aroused citizenship. The fight was started in 1919 by Arthur T. Vanderbilt, then a young lawyer and law professor thirty years old, now president of the American Bar Association. Very few of the young people know that Cincinnati was transformed, in an almost incredibly short time, from the worst governed city in the United States, termed corrupt and contented, to one of the best governed cities in our country, and that good government has prevailed there for more than twelve years. The youth of the country should be made acquainted with fine local governments, at various times, in New York, Cleveland, Milwaukee, Toledo, and other cities, large and small of the United States. They should read articles like "The City of Fallen Angels" in the *Forum* (May 1938). And where good government achieved has lagged, faltered, and been overthrown, they should be shown what were the reasons for such recessions.

The technique of political gangs in local communities is pretty uniform. It consists of open defiance of the merit system and the levying of campaign contributions in the guise of voluntary payments on the helpless adherents of political organizations. There is widespread corruption in elections. In one city, not so long ago, 199 workers in both parties were indicted and more than fifty convicted. The criminal element in the community is often in league with the political machine and gains protection in trade for campaign contributions and help at the polls. Contracts are awarded on the basis of favoritism and with disregard of the lowest and best bidder. Much of the time of the officers and officials is occupied with the machinations of politics, instead of the public business for which they are paid. The maintenance of local gangs at the expense of the public is both costly and perilous, dangerous to the community and dangerous to the country.

The fight for clean government in any community is always a difficult one; but it can succeed, partially at least, if youth enters into it whole-heartedly and as a high moral obligation. Montaigne (who, by the way, was once Mayor of Bordeaux), said: "I am of opinion that the most honorable calling is to serve the public and to be useful to the many." Instead of the spirit of cynicism, aloofness, and helplessness in local affairs that pervades the young of this country, they should be invested with something of the fervor of Charles XII of Sweden, who, in 1688, before the battle of Narva, told that the enemy were three to one, rejoined, he was glad, because then there would be enough to kill, enough to take prisoner and enough to run away. Or, if the young paladins fear failure of their effort, they should re-read their Stevenson and memorize his words "Our business in the world is not to succeed, but to continue to fail, in good spirits."

Besides, no movement for good government is ever a complete failure. Even if the effort appears to be such, something has been accomplished and if, after good government has been achieved, it should not persist, some residuum of accomplishment and betterment will remain. Hence, the youth who truly desire to be patriotic will give freely of their strength and ability for the better ordering of the affairs of the community in which they live.

-»»-»»-»»-»»-»»-»»««-«««-«««-«««-«««-«««-

29

Causes of Legal Aid Need Should

Be Attacked

(JULY 25, 1938)

*This address was delivered during a meeting of the
Legal Aid Section, American Bar Association, in
Washington, D.C., and this summary of it appears in
the Journal of the American Judicature Society, Vol.
23, No. 1 (June 1939), p. 16. Mr. Seasongood's first
contact with legal aid was while he was still in the
law school, with the New York Legal Aid Society.
He was president of the Cincinnati Legal Aid Society from 1930 to 1938; also Chairman of the Committee on Legal Aid, Cincinnati Bar Association.*

*For further comment on this subject, see his re-
view of* Legal Aid, *by Robert Egerton, in the* Harvard Law Review, *Vol. 60, No. 5 (May 1947), p. 852.
Mr. Seasongood was president of the National Legal
Aid Association from 1945 to 1948, and has been for
some time one of its two honorary vice-presidents.
At the Thirty-seventh Annual Legal Aid and Defender (the association's new name) Conference at
Cincinnati, Oct. 9, 1959, he was given the Reginald
H. Smith Medal with a citation for "dedicated
service."*

WITH ALL the changes that have come about since my
apprenticeship in legal aid in 1902, one wonders why the
Cincinnati Legal Aid Society should still be running

through the mill, each year, its 6,000 or more civil cases and the several hundred criminal cases of its voluntary defender. Since the turn of the century we have acquired social-security laws, old-age pensions, unemployment insurance, the NLRB, and, to do away with the horrors of the "fellow servant rule" and "assumption of risk," workmen's-compensation laws. We have acquired also through WPA and PWA relief even to the extent of providing clothing: transportation in some cities (New York, e. g.) at far less than cost; blue-sky laws to prevent investment in unsound securities; declaratory judgments and arbitration and small-claims courts; and teachers' and employees' credit companies. And yet the grind of cases seems to continue unabated and, indeed, to increase.

Must not, then, the legal-aid enthusiast look to the *causes* of the cases coming in and seek to remedy those causes, rather than only to apply the palliative of help for the clients? The ideal legal-aid society, or, to be specific, the National Association of Legal Aid organizations, should, in my opinion, seek to *diminish the causes* of controversies in which legal-aid organizations are asked to act. I present some subjects which are worthy of study and possibly action:

First: Sickness insurance and insurance for hospital care. The question of socialized or co-operative medicine is too large a subject for discussion here. But I became convinced, while one of the trustees of the Julius Rosenwald Fund, of the value of properly managed insurance for sickness and hospital care, especially after visiting the Negro hospital in New Orleans, entirely staffed by Negroes. That system is followed there with the greatest success, and childbirth is handled under the best and most sanitary methods, with instruction to the mother which benefits her and her child throughout life.

Second: The same for dental treatment and general adoption of rulings and legislation intended to curb the injury and awful expense incident to the activities of disreputable practitioners. In *Dr. Bloom Dentist, Inc., v. Cruise, City Clerk* (1932) 259 N.Y. 358; dismissed for want of a substantial federal question (1933), 288 U.S. 588, the city clerk was held to be within his rights in refusing a permit for a large dental electric advertising sign of a misleading character, although the application had been approved by the superintendent of buildings and commissioner of electricity as to size, etc. In *Semler v. Oregon Dental Commission,* (1935), 294 U.S. 608, a law prohibiting advertising by dentists and allowing revocation of license for nonprofessional conduct including such advertising, even though the advertising was not deceptive, was sustained.

Third: Constant and more searching investigation of all kinds of insurance than is afforded by state authorities is necessary. The expense in some small-payment companies is inordinate and such companies are badly conducted with insufficient regulation.

Fourth: Loan companies, pawn brokers, and professional bondsmen are common causes of financial distress. Statutes sometimes permit municipal pawn shops (e. g. former Ohio General Code secs. 4205—et seq., now repealed), and there are, of course, loan companies of a fine character, such as the Provident Loan Society of New York (346 Fourth Avenue) and The Citizens Loan Association of Cincinnati.

Fifth: What shall be said of installment buying? It stimulates demand by making possible purchase of numerous articles that would be impossible to acquire otherwise; but it is a frequent cause of distress. Legislation to curb night selling of jewelry at auction has been upheld. *Gordon v. City of Indianapolis* (1932) 204 Ind. 79; *Perry Trading Co. v. City of Tallahassee* (1937), . . . Fla. . . . , 174 So. 854, 111 A. L. R. 463. But not only are the older kinds of purchases, such as furniture, houses, and jewelry, still bought by the installment method, but there are radios, automobiles, watches, and clocks, dress suits, dresses, cloaks, and furs, and even razors so purchasable. Mr. Jesse Jones of Regional Finance Corporation has recently stated he wishes to force banks to undertake direct installment business instead of limiting their business, as heretofore, to customers wishing to engage in such business.

Sixth: Automobile insurance should everywhere be compulsory, and not to have driving tests and licensing of drivers is really outrageous. How many times has it happened that a wage earner, through no fault of his, is deprived of his means of livelihood, temporarily or permanently, by a wholly irresponsible moron using an automobile? Also, the habit of "fixing" citations for violations of traffic laws is a cause of a great number of violations and danger to individuals.

Seventh: The whole system of treatment of crime is hopelessly archaic. There is very little sensible attempt to rehabilitate the criminal and to allow him to readjust himself as a wage earner and supporter of a family.

Eighth: What shall we say of gambling, now largely utilized for "religious" and kindred purposes? Whether and to what extent this natural proclivity should be allowed is a subject for more consideration than it is receiving. But, certainly, if it is allowed, it should be under government supervision as in the case of European countries. Anything is better than nonenforcement and the collusion between criminals and low political gangs.

Ninth: More education and much more adult education is needed. Prevalence of existing crime has often been found due to malefactors having no skills for legitimate employment. Prostitution is an example. With better education, too, there would be better government, and there is no doubt that the defective local government that pervades most of the United States results in less use of public resources for the benefit of the localities and of those in it most in need.

Tenth: Finally, there should be a steady effort to reduce the cost of funerals and burials. Cities may conduct cemeteries (e. g. Ohio General Code Sec. 4154— et seq.). I remember one of my first cases was for the widow of an engineer killed by the escape of ammonia fumes. She had an infant child, and he left her $500, $495 of which was used by her for his funeral. Burial insurance, carried by many, is unduly expensive and results in extravagance in death out of all relation to the customary expenditures during life. Many cemetery associations also degenerate into rackets.

You may say that all this is a very ambitious program and that, as someone said of Edward Everett Hale, "His specialty is the universe." My much esteemed friend, Reginald H. Smith of Boston (almost the embodiment of legal aid) said at the 1916 meeting of the Legal Aid Societies in Cincinnati: "The legal aid society cannot undertake to reform the world." While I differ with him on legal aid or any other matter with trepidation, still I make bold to ask "Why not?" or at least why should not legal-aid societies do something of that kind, instead of merely attending to the cases that come before them? Valuable as is legal aid for the poor, the prevention, so far as possible of the necessity for it, is of even greater worth.

➤➤➤➤➤➤➤➤➤➤➤➤➤◄◄◄◄◄◄◄◄◄◄◄◄◄

30

Some Changes in Law

(APRIL 15, 1939)

*Mr. Seasongood's address was delivered at the law
section annual meeting of the Associated Harvard
Clubs in New Orleans, and is reprinted from a report of the proceedings in the* Harvard Alumni Bulletin, *Oct. 1939. (Supporting legal authorities there
cited are not printed here.)*

THANK YOU, Mr. Chairman, for your kind words of introduction. I never knew, until I got into political controversies, what a calm and peaceful pursuit the law is.
To be able to talk on something unrelated to politics is a
pleasure. I feel pretty old as I stand here and recall John
Chipman Gray having spoken at the Law School and
having said: "I am the prehistoric man. I shall not call
you brethren; I shall call you friends." When I see all
these younger men here, I think I, too, am in that situation; and I have some hesitancy, of course, being just a
run-of-the-mine lawyer, in following the brilliant Dean of
the Harvard Law School. But I feel better about it after
having read, in one of the late Mr. Justice Holmes's
papers, of the experience of Sir Edward Coke. He married the Lady Hatton without banns or license in a private house and incurred possible excommunication by the
Archbishop. A number of other great legal personages

also were present, and they all, by their proctor, accepted censure, on the ground that the offense had been committed through ignorance of law. I do not know whether the lady was related to Hatton, the famous dancing chancellor of Queen Elizabeth. I do not suppose she was, because we must remember Coke's aversion to what he thought were incursions of equity on the common law. He would not have had a union with equity, even in the state of marriage.

I should like to call attention to some of the profound changes that have occurred since I began the study of law. Of course, that is a long time back and there was room for a good many changes; but they have been of an extraordinary character. Some have already been mentioned by the dean (Dean James M. Landis of the Harvard Law School). I advert to the changes first in the mechanical world which have had a tendency to influence and revolutionize the practice of law. Just before I came down here, I happened across a case which involved the question of whether there could be a property right in an electrical transcription of the performance by the plaintiff's orchestra of a piece called "Wahoo." This plaintiff had developed a particular style for his orchestra, and had limited the production of that "Wahoo." Well, the question came up as to what restrictions you could have, not on personal property, but on something so intangible as your particular method of playing a particular piece, and it was held that the plaintiff was entitled to protection. Also, it is interesting that the judge cited five different law-review articles in support of the conclusion he reached. Forty years ago that would not have been apt to occur.

You perhaps recall the recent aviation case where there was some limitation on the old rule that if you owned the land, you owned up to the heavens and down to the reverse. That does not obtain any more according to this decision, where some persons flew over complainant's land at heights of from 150 down to ten feet. The court said that ownership to the heavens does not exist except in a very qualified way, and denied relief.

Still more recent are parking meters. Just in the last *Law Week* you have the case of *Gilsey Building, Inc., v. the incorporated Village of Great Neck Plaza.* The lot owner there complained that the placing of parking meters in front of his property deprived him of some of his rights, and it could not be done; but the courts said that it could.

Now, I have called your attention to some mechanical inventions which have caused litigation. There are radio, motion pictures, television, aviation, and the automobile. Of course all these new instrumentalities have resulted in new conceptions of law and new thinking about law.

The dean has also referred to legislation, and I fear it is true that with us of the older school there is a certain hostility to legislation. We do not like this encroachment on the law as we learned it. I think it was Dean Pound who said that the common-law lawyer is at his worst when approaching legislation and the study of legislation. Mr. Justice Stone, at the Harvard Law School Tercentenary celebration, bade us be hospitable to legislation, and interpret it as an aid in the development of law.

The dean has mentioned some of the extraordinary happenings in this third of a century.

Now we have workmen's compensation, legal aid, and public defenders. We have taxes of great variety: income, estate, gift, sales, and processing taxes, and the number can be greatly added to. Domestic Relations courts are new things in this century, some including also the treatment of the juvenile delinquent. You have blue-sky and fair-trade laws, Social Security, old-age pensions, unemployment and workmen's-compensation insurance, arbitration, declaratory judgments, small claims and conciliation courts. There is the important question of installment buying, credit agencies, and, if I may revert to my particular favorite, municipal government. I suppose I am like some man Lord Chesterfield used to tell about. When he wanted to divert the conversation to fire arms, he would bang on the table and say: "That sounds like a gun. I remember when I was hunting," and so on. And, sooner or later, I bang on the table and shout: "Local government!"

The greatest changes have perhaps occurred in this field of municipal law. Now you have home rule for many, not enough cities; you have the growth of the merit system—too slow, regrettably; initiative and referendum; excess condemnation. I hasten to say that does not mean of civic officials. You have setbacks; that is, when the city thinks it is going to widen a street at some time in the future, and it is not desirable that apartment houses or office buildings be erected up to the lot line, and later condemned, the public officials establish a set-back line to hold the property back until such time as the condemnation takes place, thus eliminating the expense incident to appropriating a new building. May that be done without compensation? Or, must the owner be compensated for the restricted use of his property? You have a flock of cases and decisions in connection with planning and zoning. They are all creations of this century, and the most recent arrival is the freeway.

The first statute passed in connection with the establishment of freeways was in Rhode Island in 1937. The freeway, in the interest of through traffic, cuts off the rights of the abutter, including the right of access. It establishes a through traffic street, and does not allow the abutter to have direct access to that street. That leads to many new legal questions, as you can imagine.

You also have municipal ownership of public utilities and public housing. So, I repeat, we are in a period of very great change in the law.

When, in 1932, I was a member of President Hoover's Housing Conference, I was assigned, with two others, to write on the legal aspects of the problem, and we reached the conclusion, in accordance with the decisions at the time, that probably it could not be done by the Federal government. I feel a little more comfortable about that, because our Court of Appeals for the Sixth Circuit later reached the same conclusion. That was on a limited view of what constitutes a public use, and of the general welfare clause. Now, of course, that is all swept into the discard. I do not believe that anybody thinks that way any more. If he does, it does him no good. Now you have cases, and the most recent ones are the City of Muncie, Indiana, and that of Peoria, Illinois, and there are many others all saying such housing is permissible.

The question is, with these new revolutionary changes, new social thinking, and new mechanical developments,

how much is going to be left of our old common law?
Well, a certain amount will persist. Sir Frederick Pollock
has referred to the earliest recorded case which is still
authority, and that is the leading case of Zelophehad's
daughters (Numbers 27:7 and 8). I do not know
whether that means anything to you. Anyway, they succeeded, by a plea to Moses, in inheriting from their
father who had no sons.

I was just recently reading how Daniel did a pretty
good piece of legal work in demanding a separation of
the witnesses. I do not know whether that practice obtains in the civil law or not. Daniel found it extremely
valuable in behalf of the chaste Susanna against the
testimony of the elders. The people were about to stone
her to death, and Daniel asked the elders separately
where the alleged act took place. One said under the
holm tree; the other asserted it was under the mastic
tree. This conflicting evidence resulted in the stoning to
death of the elders instead. At this late date it is not
appropriate to question whether is it essential under
which tree an act took place, if it did, or whether it
might have taken place under both trees? This separation
of the witnesses is a valuable thing undoubtedly. The
law is still encumbered with a lot of moss, verbiage, and
poor stuff that should be cut away. I was reading recently Mr. McCarter's *Memories of Half a Century at
the New Jersey Bar*, in which he refers to the case of *Coke
v. Shinkle* in early Vroom. There the plaintiff suing in
trover alleged "he had casually lost from his messuage a
barn, which the defendant had casually found and ap-
propriated to his own use."

Speaking again of Coke's marriage outside of the

159

church, it is a quaint bit of formalism that while burglary had, at common law, to be a breaking into and entering an inhabited mansion or dwelling house in the night season, etc., it was possible to commit burglary in an empty church, because the church was the dwelling house of God.

I wish to discuss with you for a moment the lessened adherence in our law to the rule of *stare decisis* and, in the civil law, to the rule of *jurisprudence constante*. The difference, I have recently learned, between the two is that in the former, if there is a single case squarely in point, it is the duty of the court to follow that decision. The latter requires more than that. There must be a combination of decisions in point before they have binding effect. Well, there certainly is a tendency to get away from the binding effect of precedent both in the common and in the civil law, and I think it is well that we should not continue to have that slavish adherence which led someone to say: "The appellate court corrects the errors of inferior tribunals and perpetuates its own."

The dean has referred to administrative tribunals. They have a great effect in lessening the influence of the rule of *stare decisis*. A good many of them do not have that rule at all. The Interstate Commerce Commission, as I understand it, is not bound by previous decisions, and a good many of them do not have any rule on the subject, and there is also a letting down of established rules of evidence.

One other consideration that to my mind will make for a lessening of adherence to the rule of *stare decisis* is the bringing into judicial positions and into public administration of law professors. There have been a great many of those recently appointed, and they are going to affect the law very much. I can speak somewhat freely about law professors, because I am a kind of one myself. I do think they have a certain *guadium certaminis*. They like to argue, and they do not believe that an ounce of precedent is worth a pound of principle; an interesting inquiry is how these men will shape the law as it goes along. They are mostly young men, and have a long time in which to shape it.

I wonder whether this striking difference elucidated by Dean Pound—"Civil law is the law of the universities; its oracles always have been the teachers. Common law is the law of the courts; its oracles always have been the judges"—will persist. Of course, in some continental systems, persons study to be judges and never practice at the bar; but it comes as a little shock to some of us, to have this large body of judges without experience of practice, or even judicial experience, put in important places on the bench. I certainly hope that what Dean Pound also said, that "in the Roman Law, the judge is a part of the administrative hierarchy, whereas in the common law he is independent" will not change for us, and that it will never be any different.

Reverting to *stare decisis*, it never was an absolute postulate, even in the common law. Coke, Blackstone, and others all said that a judge may rightfully refuse to follow a precedent which is absurd, contrary to reason, or plainly inconvenient. That would seem to give a considerable latitude. Mr. Justice Holmes said, "it is revolting to have no better reason for a rule of law than that it was so laid down in the time of Henry IV."

Of course, adherence to the rule of *stare decisis* originated in England, and there is a reason why they adhere to it closely there. It is a habit we fall into, to follow what somebody else has done somewhere else, without considering whether or not our conditions are comparable. Now, Lord Wright, at this same Tercentenary conference, mentioned that in England they have a Law Revision Committee, and that wherever there is a decision that seems bad in effect, or not in accordance with good and established practice, the Law Revision Committee recommends a statutory amendment, and it is put through parliament as a nonpolitical measure.

The late Mr. Justice Cardozo recommended something of the same sort in an article in the *Harvard Law Review* in 1921, and Dean Pound has also spoken in favor of such committees; but they have eventuated only in New York in 1934, and I believe they just passed something of the kind in Louisiana. Judicial councils deal only with matters of procedure and the business of the courts, but Law Revision Committees furnish a method of getting statutory cure of decisions which seem inadequate.

I shall not dilate on the recently enlarged meaning, through decisions of the U.S. Supreme Court, of the commerce and general-welfare clauses, but I cannot help referring to an expansion of the rule of proximate cause which seems to me to be a proper overruling of old doctrine. It is in the Lanasa fruit case decided in 1938, and as it deals with bananas, it perhaps has a good deal of local interest. In that case, the insurance was marine insurance, and the cargo was a cargo of bananas which would have ordinarily got to their destination all right, but the vessel stranded and the bananas deteriorated. The insurance company set up that the bananas had an inherent vice. Of course, I knew there was some inherent vice about the original apple, but that a banana has any particular vice I did not know before, unless the skin happened to be in an inappropriate place on the side-walk. At all events the rule had been, under the English marine-insurance cases, that that inherent vice was the proximate cause of the destruction of the cargo, and not the stranding of the vessel. Mr. Chief Justice Hughes swept that aside, and said that the real, efficient cause was the stranding of the vessel, and it recalled to me a lit-tle verse we used to sing at the Law School:

> *The natural and probable it is the rule today.*
> *The but for rule it is no good,*
> *It has long since passed away.*
> *The natural and proximate will be the rule some*
>   *day,*
> *For so says Jere Smith.*
>   Chorus:
> *Jere, Jere, Jeremiah and the late Chief Justice Doe!*
> *(for whom Jerry had an almost idolatrous venera-*
> *tion)*

The most striking case, of course, that occurs to one is *Erie Railroad Co. v. Tompkins.* I had a certain affec-tion for *Swift v. Tyson* because, for some fool reason, I could always remember the citation, 16 Peters 1. Al-though the case once cost a client of mine a good deal of money, I, like other old-timers, had got used to it and had accepted as a settled rule that the Federal courts would determine for themselves in commercial cases what was the law of the state in which they happened to be sitting. Now that hundred-year precedent is overruled by *Erie Railroad Co. v. Tompkins.*

Last summer, at the International Congress of Comparative Law at The Hague, I had a very entertaining conversation with Sir Maurice Amos. He was seventy years old and retired, but was taking up anew study of the Constitution of the United States. He insisted there is a common law of the United States, and to prove it relied upon *Swift v. Tyson.* I said: "No, the federal judges are just determining what the law of a State is, and they think they know it better than the judges of the State know it." The late Dean Wald of the Cincinnati Law School said that there is only one instance on record where anybody convinced anybody else in an argument, and in that case there were two brothers who used to debate protection and free trade. They convinced each other, and so the debate went on from opposite sides. At all events, when this decision came out, I took malicious pleasure in sending it to Sir Maurice. He wrote back: "If your Supreme Court was going to overrule the multiplication table and the Ten Commandments, and *Swift v. Tyson,* they might at least have done so before my book appeared from the press."

It is too hot and too late to go into what I intended to discuss at some length, namely, the altered view of the United States Supreme Court on intersovereign tax immunity; . . .

Anyway, we can no longer enjoy the comfortable

theory we used to have represented by the Lord Chancellor's caroling in *Iolanthe:*

> *The law is the true embodiment of everything that's excellent. It has no kind of fault or flaw. And I, my lords, embody the law.*

A good many of us feel like the old gentleman who said when the Field Code was passed in New York that "they had repealed everything he knew." I think we shall have to pull ourselves together and keep alert.

There is one other thing I should like to say before stopping. These administrative tribunals are here. It is just silly to have toward them the attitude Coke had toward equity; they are going to stay here so long as any of us will know anything about law. But one of the great weaknesses of them is that they, in many instances, have in their personnel some who have not been put there by reason of merit. As long as we have administrative tribunals, why should there not be insistence by the lawyers that legal positions be filled under the Merit System? Why should we not add to the effectiveness of administrative tribunals by having them recruited on the basis of merit, so that they may function well and bring about changes that are necessary? Also, all of this rotten stuff of favoritism in appointments of referees and appraisers on a political basis must likewise be done away with.

Now, I have not given you very good reasons for what I have been trying to say, like the doctor who filled in a death certificate, and inadvertently wrote his name in the blank as the cause of death. The health official, a very considerate person, said no doubt the reason was true, but could not the physician give a more scientific explanation. I hope I shall not have the experience, either, of the fusty old barrister whose wig was awry. Observing those in the courtroom laughing at him, he asked of Curran: "Do you observe anything ridiculous in this wig?" To which Curran replied: "Only the head."

⋙⋙⋙⋙⋙⋙⋘⋘⋘⋘⋘⋘⋘

31

Medes and Persians Law—Does It Still Exist?

(OCTOBER 1940)

This address, delivered at the Ohio State Bar Association Junior Bar Section luncheon in Cincinnati, is reprinted from the full report in the Ohio Bar, *Vol. 13, No. 42 (Jan. 6, 1941), p. 577. For another address along somewhat similar lines, see "Was Coke Right?" delivered at a meeting of the Indiana State Bar Association at Indianapolis, Jan. 16, 1937, printed in the* Indiana Law Journal, *Vol. 12, No. 4 (Apr. 1937), p. 247. Mr. Seasongood was a member of the Ohio Commission of Code Revision from 1945 to 1949.*

THE PRESIDENT introduced the speaker after reading the following telegram:

Honorable Murray Seasongood, Speakers Table. We suppose you fellows liked Harvard:—one man's mede is another man's persian. (Signed) Yale Table.

Mr. Chairman, Members of the Junior Bar, with whom I include, of course, such juniors as Mr. President of the American Bar, Mr. President of the Ohio State

Bar, and other distinguished ladies and gentlemen present:

This is a typical Yale Law School telegram: it is incomprehensible. It shows that the senders were under the influence of Mr. Rodell, who wrote the book *Woe Unto Ye Lawyers*.

I suppose the Yale people don't know what the laws of the Medes and Persians are. Doubtless it is not polite for me to say I tried out the ones on my left and my right and none of them seemed to know. One of them thought it had something to do with an eye for an eye and a tooth for a tooth. . . .

There was a report this morning of the American Bar Association meeting by Mr. Barkdull; but he neglected to tell about an episode when he and our president, Mr. Fredriks, and Jim Logue and I went out to the magnificent estate of the duPonts. We had dinner, 500 of us, in the conservatory, and the rest of the bar, while we ate, had their hungry faces pressed against the glass of the conservatory and got nothing to eat and said: "Instead of all these beautiful orchids, they ought to have a hot-dog stand on the place." Anyway, we four were able to sit down, and I sat on a chair that collapsed like the one-horse shay; and later I went home in a bus and I sat in the bus and that broke down; and then I had to transfer to another bus, and as it was crowded and there were no hand holds, I wobbled around a good deal, and lurched on the laps of most of the ladies in the bus, and they broke down; and so I suppose the managers here thought I am less likely to do injury on my feet, even if talking, than if permitted to sit and listen to somebody else.

This title presupposes that you know something about the Bible, and I won't assume you are like Sir John Simon's friend who, asked to explain the difference between the cherubim and seraphim, said: "There used to be a difference between them, but they made it up.". . .

Anyway, this text (Daniel 6:12–24), if you choose to call it that, is from the fact that when Darius was King, there were certain people who didn't like Daniel, and caused the King to pass a statute or a decree that anybody who prayed except to the King would be thrown to the lions; and they told Darius when Daniel did it: "The law of the Medes and Persians is that no decree or statute which the King establisheth may be changed." And so the statement has come to be that "the law of the Medes and Persians changeth not." But, curiously, it did change, even in that particular instance, and in a very illogical and somewhat unfair manner; because when the lions refused to perform with Daniel, all of his accusers, their wives and children, were thrown to the lions in his place, and that seems to have been some modification of the law which doesn't appear in the statute itself.

Now, is our law at the present time as rigid and inflexible and unchanging as this law of the Medes and Persians which changeth not? Certainly not in the domain of constitutional law. In fact, the changes are, for me, much too rapid, and I think some of you may have heard Dean Landis mention that the course on constitutional law at his law school is no longer referred to as such, but as current events.

I have tried to summarize what constitutional law under the new order is now, and it is, in brief, that everything is constitutional. (That is the way it is in

England, of course, and has been, but it is being made that way here by court decision now.) Everything is taxable, everything is interstate commerce except the *Apex Hosiery* case (309 U.S. 644), and everything that an administrative tribunal does is all right.

Recently there was a decision, by a lower court in New York, it is true, but a very interesting decision, on the validity of limitations of price on theater tickets, and you remember that the old *Tyson* case (273 U.S. 418) was to the effect that that was an attempt to regulate an industry not affected with a public interest and was therefore invalid. Now comes this New York court (9 U.S.L.W. 2227, Oct. 15, 1940), and says, based on the *Nebbia v. New York* case (291 U.S. 502), the milk-marketing case in the U.S. Supreme Court, that the old conception of public interest is no longer operative, but if the Legislature has power to legislate on the subject at all they may legislate in such way as seems to them appropriate and proper. So there, as I say, is fundamental change in a doctrine of constitutional law.

When you come to evidence, I heard a distinguished former Federal judge, Judge Patterson, a very able man, now Assistant Secretary of War, say just recently he thought evidence was on the way out, that all these rules that have been built up over so many years are to disappear within the next twenty-five years or in a shorter period. There are these ferments and changes then in certain aspects of the law.

But do we realize how much need there is of change in matters of procedure and other aspects of law? Again referring to Sir John Simon, he said here in Cincinnati, when Attorney General of England, that the law was never a bed of roses: it was either all bed and no roses for those who didn't get business, or all roses and no bed for those who did. Well, that to some extent is the difficulty in trying to get these changes that are necessary in the interest of simplification, of lessening of expense, of modernizing and of making the law a working instrument suitable for the habits of our daily lives. The younger men are scratching around making a living and getting ahead. The older practitioners who have been successful or moderately so say: "Well, this is a pretty good institution because it has made us successful, and we are not in favor of any change."

Let us consider Lord Eldon, of whom we speak with so much reverence and yet of whom it was said by Bagehot that it is impossible to conceive there was such a man. He was opposed to anything in the way of innovation or change; he was opposed to parliamentary reform, he was opposed to modification of the rigors of the common law, he was opposed to lessening the number of capital offenses, he was the ideal and complete standpatter of his time, and because he ran the whole affair (others appeared to be prime minister, but he was the real power behind the throne), he was opposed to any change at all.

We start in with a false premise when we assert that law is the perfection of reason. That is not a good starting point, because the minute you are so fond of yourself or anything else, you don't become critical. We should rather have the idea that law is not the perfection of reason and that there is a lot that needs constant change and modification if it is to be made anything that approximates perfection. I think much better is Bacon's *Ad-*

vancement of Learning, wherein he says: "If we begin with certainties we shall end with doubts, but if we begin with doubts we shall end in certainties." And I don't like the attitude of that English judge who said: "I may be wrong, but I am never in doubt."

Now, in brief, what are some of the things that need changing? There are a whole lot of them which have troubled me from time to time, and I shan't keep you so long as to wear you out, I hope, but long enough only to mention a few, some which I may have already advanced to members of this association on other occasions. This large audience, I think, must be proof, however, that a considerable number who are here have not heard me before.

Well, why don't we have a deed in simple form? What is the use of having all of these covenants in a deed? Why can't you have it established that a deed that says "I grant" necessarily contains all usual covenants and warranties just as much as if they were written out?

Why can't you have a simple form of judgment? I have seen judgments in other states, not so much in this state, where they recite everything that happened from the beginning of the world in the judgment. No sense in it. Why don't you just have "judgment affirmed" or "judgment reversed" and that is all there is to it?

Why don't you have a simple form of mandate instead of sending greetings down to the person who is licked? Why don't we have simple forms of writs? Again, even if you are not astute, you know you have been sued if they tell you so. And why don't we use the mails? Why don't we modernize, ladies and gentlemen? Here are the mails we use for the most important things: we don't have to have riding deputies any more as they did in the old days. If you would get a communication coming from the common-pleas court or from any other tribunal, you would look to see what it is. They have used the mails effectively for the service of summons in Cleveland by rule of the municipal court. There is a city with a large shifting population of diverse elements, and my information is that it has been used with entire success. Now we have to reduce the expense of litigation and make it more consistent with the general ideas of the people.

Then why should you have affidavits except for the benefit of hungry notaries public? In Massachusetts, if you sign a statement, the statutory requirements are that you are subject to punishment of perjury if it isn't so. If you put yourself down in black and white, why isn't that enough, and what is the difference whether you swear to it or not? You know how those affidavits are regarded. You know the story of the important businessman who was signing papers right along without reading them, and his secretary said: "You had better read that one, it is a statement to the bank." "Oh," he said, "I thought it was an affidavit."

What about the doctrine of consideration? That is an obsolete idea to my mind. It does not exist in the civil law. There again, if you put yourself down in black and white with the intention of contracting, what is the use of having the books cluttered up with questions of consideration? Lord Mansfield tried to get rid of it as far back as 1760 without success, and Lord Wright, as you may have seen in his articles, is still trying to insist (and a great many people feel the same way) that you would get rid of a lot of litigation and fine distinctions if you abolish the whole doctrine of consideration and say as people ordinarily believe, and let the doctrine approach ordinary morality, that if you put yourself down in black and white and promise something, you ought to stick to that promise.

I think we should have in Ohio, as we have in the Federal courts, permission to appeal from an order granting or dissolving a preliminary injunction. In the Federal courts, you can appeal from an order granting or allowing a preliminary injunction, and the court of appeals in certain instances will dismiss the whole case in such an appeal and get through with the thing. (*Lyons v. Empire Fuel Co.*, 262 F. 465, Sixth Circuit.) Why not? Why doesn't that prevent the unnecessary protraction of the case and additional expense and time for the courts and for the litigants?

I think we have to revise our thoughts about transactions with a person deceased. . . .

Another matter we have in our Ohio law—these are just a few of a great number that have been on my mind which I won't bore you with, save one or two more—is our wrongful death statute. If a man is killed and leaves a widow dependent on him for support, and she brings the suit (as was the case in some litigation with which we were connected), and an instructed defendant's verdict is taken to the Supreme Court and reversed, and in the meantime the widow dies and there is nobody left who was dependent upon the man who was killed—I don't want to say this absolutely because I may want to make the opposite contention, I say this like the young man Guppy used to write his love letters, "without prejudice"—it appears, though the Ohio law is that, as there is then no one remaining who is dependent for support, there is no cause of action remaining. Now, why shouldn't the action, if it was a good one when the dame was alive, remain an asset of her estate? I present that to you for consideration.

Then I should like to sweep away, as I have been trying for many years (the *Virginia Law Review*, Vol. 22, p. 910), all this nonsense about governmental and proprietary capacity in municipal corporations. I won't do more than say that there has been a great amount written on that and we talk about it, but it is being whittled away very slowly in the decisions.

And then why don't we recognize that aesthetics is a proper subject of legal protection in these days? You read the letters of the late Justice Holmes. He said he approached the matter gingerly in some case in Massachusetts (*Hubbard v. Tomlinson*, 140 Mass. 467, 468), and then again in the *St. Louis Billboard* case (249 U.S. 269, 274). You have to approach it by stealth: that is the only way you can get it into the law. Now, why isn't that a legitimate subject of legal protection? If the nose is entitled to protection against evil smells and the ear against cacophonous sounds, why isn't the eye entitled to be represented in a court of law and have some protection for aesthetics and the beautifying of the communities in which we live?

Now I call for changes and an open mind on things that we take for granted because we are working under a system and we haven't much time to think about it.

175

The lawyers have always been ultraconservative, if I may say so. There was too much formalism in the law in old times, and still is.

I don't know if you ever saw the writ in the clerk's office at Salem, Massachusetts, and the return of it where it says: "In obedience to the above writ I took the said Bridget Bishop from His Majesty's gaol the 16th of August, 1692, to the place of execution and hanged her by the neck until she was dead and buried." Then he saw he had made it a little strong, and he struck "buried" through with his pen. That shows the state of excitement that existed, and perhaps in the case of witches it is not fair to say that the lawyers were any more conservative about belief in them than anybody else, since the statute abolishing witchcraft as a crime was not passed until about 1740.

Blackstone said that it was very humane of the common law to drag a person who was convicted of treason to the place of execution on a hurdle instead of on the roadway itself. He gave that as an instance of the humanity of the common law, although you know the dreadful sentence that was imposed. . . . Filthy prisons and sponging houses were utilized for imprisonment for debt. It took Erskine to persuade Lord Eldon and George III and to vindicate the rights of speech and of printing and of a citizen to speak the truth.

Well, you may say: "That is all changed, those are habits that have long gone out of usage, we lawyers at the present time don't have anything of that kind." And yet if you read Lord MacMillan's book, you will see how words of art were until recently a necessity, and in the Scottish law it was necessary to use the word "dispone" to convey a good title, and if you didn't use that word "dispone," no matter if you used any other words, you didn't convey a good title, and that was true until 1874. And in the English law if you conveyed title in fee, it wasn't a good conveyance of a fee unless you actually used the words "in fee simple," and that was decided in 1901. And of course permitting an accused to have counsel or to testify in his own behalf didn't come about in England until later, I believe, around 1898.

Now in our own country . . . I recommend, if you haven't read it, Auerbach's *The Bar of Other Days*. One of his chapters is on David Dudley Field and the difficulties he had in getting his code adopted and doing away with the old forms of action in this country, particularly in New York, where he started and labored for twelve years unremittingly before he accomplished that. He says:

> *It will surprise many a practitioner of today to know that before joinder of issues, instead of the present-day simple procedure, there could be a declaration—our complaint—the plea—our answer—the replication—our reply; rejoinder, answer to reply; surrejoinder, answer to answer to reply; rebutter, answer to answer to answer to reply; and surrebutter; and on occasion still other pleadings.*

Yet, all the men who practiced under that system thought that it was all right, they didn't see anything wrong with it, and therefore I suggest for all of us to have an attitude of criticism, of critical analysis of everything that we do in the law to see whether it is right. What is

177

right, let's hold to and preserve at all costs, but whatever should be done away with, let's do away with. I can still remember, although it is ever so many years ago, when I first started the practice of law, that the Ohio Supreme Court decided, I should say, about three fourths of the cases without report. They sat in two sections. You never knew what hit you or what hit the other fellow, because the "opinions" read either affirmed or reversed without report. And when there was some agitation among the lawyers to urge the judges of the Supreme Court to give reasons for their decision, which of course are not only satisfying to the litigant who wins, but help the court itself to reach a right conclusion, many leading members of the bar were inflexible against anything of that kind and said that it was discourteous to the court to make any such suggestion.

All I have tried to indicate is that we mustn't be too self-satisfied. We should look to see how we can better the profession which we love and to which we are devoted. I hope I have not been like the judge who, I suppose, is familiar to all the Cleveland lawyers. He charged learnedly and long, in an accident case, on negligence and contributory negligence, proximate cause and the last clear chance, and as the jurors were being led out, one of them said to the bailiff: "What do we do now?"

The bailiff replied: "The Judge wants you to find out who was at fault for the accident."

"Oh," he said, "is that it? Why didn't he say so?"

32

The Merit System

(MARCH 1, 1941)

*The question of whether the Merit System should
be used in making appointments of lawyers for public service was explored by Murray Seasongood at
the Cincinnati Conference on "Law and Lawyers in
the Modern World." The address is reprinted from
the Cincinnati Law Review, Vol. 15, No. 2 (1941),
p. 209. Mr. Seasongood's article entitled "The Merit
System—An Essential of Good Government" appears in the Vanderbilt Law Review, Vol. 8, No. 4
(June 1955), p. 838; his book review of The Law of
Civil Service, by H. Eliot Kaplan, appears in the
A.B.A. Journal, Vol. 45 (Feb. 1959), pp. 171–3.*

*From 1938 to 1949 he was chairman of the Ad-
visory Committee of the Ohio Civil Service Council,
and has been connected for many years with the National Civil Service League. He is now a vice-president and member of the Executive Committee; was
chairman of the American Bar Association Committee on Civil Service from 1937 to 1953; and drafted
and sponsored the two resolutions quoted in the
above address calling for the bar to uphold the
Merit System. From 1947 to 1953 he was also a
member of the U.S. Civil Service Commission
Loyalty Review Board. His article (with Richard L.
Strecker) "The Loyalty Review Board" appears in
the University of Cincinnati Law Review, Vol. 25,
No. 1 (Winter 1956), pp. 1–42.*

THE CHIEF JUSTICE got considerable entertainment this morning by referring to me as Professor. I suppose I am like the late Professor Donovan who was a retired prize fighter and taught the manly art of self-defense at Harvard. He would always say, when he told you, for instance, to parry with your palm out: "Now I will show you de philosophy of dat." And it is recounted that Professor James, when he would meet Professor Royce, liked to say: "Well, Professor, how is our colleague, Professor Donovan, this morning?" In what I am about to say, I am talking not as a two-hour-a-week professor, but, as the chairman has said, as a practitioner. It is pretty hard for a professor to compress so important and vital a subject into a quarter of an hour.

July 1, 1938, the House of Delegates of the American Bar Association unanimously adopted a resolution:

> *Resolved: It is the duty of the Bar to uphold the merit system in public employment, to seek its wider adoption and better enforcement in national, state and local governments, to demonstrate its applicability to legal positions in the public service to attract young lawyers to a career of holding legal positions in such service and to increase confidence in administrative agencies on the basis of such agencies being officered and staffed by persons appointed because of merit and divorced from suspicion of political influence.*

That, I may say, was unanimously adopted by the House of Delegates of the American Bar Association. Encouraged by that, the Section of Municipal Law had a special study made of the lawyer in the civil service—

recruitment, selection, service, and opportunity—by the secretary of the National Civil Service Reform Association, who is himself a lawyer. And he gathered a great deal of information, which is contained in a report later submitted by the Municipal Law Section, of instances of successful use of the merit system for lawyers in public employment. That is printed, and I think there are still copies available for those who may be interested.

And then at the Philadelphia meeting of the American Bar Association the House of Delegates adopted another resolution, in September 1940, in which they said:

> *Resolved, that in the opinion of this Association it is desirable that lawyers in public positions, including examiners and staffs of administrative agencies, but not including elective and policy determining heads, be employed, so far as practicable, under the merit system, with the aid of competitive examinations, and that this Association further such method of selection.*

Now, the House is a somewhat "hard-boiled" body. It is composed, as you know, of practitioners, judges, public officers, and a great variety of persons who are entitled to membership in it, and I repeat that these resolutions were adopted unanimously. May I also state that some of the most distinguished persons in the legal profession have favored this method of selection. They are not children, or theorists; they are persons who have a practical knowledge that they used when favoring this recommendation. I mention, among a great number, persons like Dean Pound, Senator George Wharton Pepper, Mr. Silas Strawn, and Mr. F. H. Stinchfield, all of whom wrote individual letters when it was thought support might be needed in aid of the resolution that was presented to the House of Delegates.

The Federal Bar Association in October 1938 approved, by a vote of its Executive Council, and then by a referendum vote of the members, extension of the Merit System to lawyers in the Federal service.

We are not dealing with something new or experimental. It may come as a surprise to some of you who have not looked into the matter greatly, to know that this system has been utilized with complete success over a long period of years. For instance, reference has been made to the Interstate Commerce Commission. They have used the Merit System, with competitive examinations, in the recruitment of the attorneys of their staff. I think most of us who have had experience with the Commission will say that the Interstate Commerce Commission personnel is as good as that of the best commissions we have dealings with. The Internal Revenue Bureau recruits its legal personnel after examination. The United States Department of Agriculture, as I know, for the period 1913 to 1917, and before that, had about fifty lawyers—the entire legal staff in the classified service, and their representation as lawyers was extremely good. The New York City Law Department is, of course, a tremendous law office, and the civil service is utilized there in, I think, about eighty-five per cent of the legal positions. The Corporation Counsel of Buffalo informed me that in that city every attorney in the Corporation Counsel's office obtained his position as the result of a competitive civil-service examination. There are many counsel in departments of the state of California who are recruited by this method. The Corporation Counsel's office in Milwaukee uses this system. And perhaps the most striking instance is that of the Corporation Counsel of Los Angeles County, California, a position which pays $10,000, and which was filled by use of competitive examination, with entire satisfaction to everybody concerned.

Now, the stock arguments against this method of recruiting lawyers in public positions by use of the Merit System and competitive examinations are due, I think, perhaps to a lack of information, because that exists, but also to considerations of politics and the desire for political patronage.

Just in the last week you may have seen the report of the President's Committee on Personnel. I saw it in one of our daily papers. And judging by that journal's references occasionally to myself, there may be some inaccuracies in that paper's report. But the report shows that while the whole committee agreed there should be a career service for lawyers in the public service, there were four who favored without qualification use of the Merit System, and the other four (I am only judging now by the newspaper report) felt that written examinations would not be suitable tests for the ascertainment of lawyers' abilities.

Well, the answer to that is that you do not depend only upon written examinations. It is a common misapprehension, and scares lawyers to death, that they are again to be subjected to a law-school examination, through which they once had perilously navigated. The general examination has to be a sensible examination, and is to be conducted as, for instance, the one in Los

Angeles County, to which I referred, by a proper examining board consisting, like as not, of judges and practitioners of great experience, with the desire of ascertaining whether the lawyer is suitable for the position. As some friend of mine said, in a certain case: "Do you want an *absque hoc* lawyer, or one who will win the case?" You do not have to have an *absque hoc* lawyer. You can consider such factors as personality and experience, and that indefinite expression, executive ability—all those things should be considered. And likewise, the appointing officer has some latitude. He has an opportunity of selection. He is not necessarily required to take the first one on the list. I do not believe there is much of a fiduciary relationship, or if there is, that is an objection to the use of the system. I do not believe that fiduciary relationship is true any more in the selection of lawyers to fill legal positions in the public service than in a great many other positions where the Merit System is used with complete success and satisfaction to all concerned. May I say that I would recognize as an exception, key men in the top positions, just as you do in other positions where you allow a man to select two or three of his principal assistants without reference to the Merit System, those to be the policy determining members of the organization. But there are a great number of lawyer positions where there is no fiduciary relationship, except fidelity to the public, and it is not at all important whether they be of the same political persuasion in national or any other politics as the chief of the section.

Let us assume there are some weaknesses in the system of competitive examinations for lawyers in public positions, as is true of any institution you may utilize. Then you have to consider the alternative, if you do not use this system.

What is the alternative? Well, it is that if you do not have a career system, if it is not possible for a man in public employment to adopt it as a career and to be selected on the basis of merit and to retain his position on the basis of merit, then you have him obtain it by the political method, and his tenure is insecure. When his political group goes out, out he goes, too. And what is the result? His loyalty is more to the particular boss or leader or head of the department than to the interests of the client he is to serve, that is to say, the public. You have a labor turnover which is disastrous from the public point of view. You have men who have acquired efficiency in the particular field; and as they are busied with the affairs of ordinary existence, bread and butter affairs, they are prone to have a kind of an eye to the possibilities of what may beckon to them after they are out of their particular position. They have no security there, and the experience they have acquired on the public's time and in public position does not then redound or continue to redound to the benefit of the public, but is rapidly taken over by the utilities or the companies which are or may be in opposition to the public in various matters that come up for solution.

And lastly, I think political selection and retention have a very debasing influence upon the practice of law. As it is now, there are a great many young lawyers who immediately link up with one or the other political organization because they have the practical certainty that when they get out they can have something thrown to them, or may acquire a position which will pay them out of all proportion to their legal ability. Well, then, they lose their interest in the law, in the ordinary way of getting ahead in the law, by study and diligence, and attention to the affairs entrusted to them, and they see their advancement is necessarily linked to the fortunes of the political organization which gave them the position. That has an unfortunate influence, in my opinion, upon the legal profession, by diverting and side-tracking these lawyers who are coming into the practice from the faithful and conscientious and laborious and often tedious study and advancement in the ordinary way in law, to advancement by the political method. And as these lawyers of the same kind become judges, you often have judges who have little sympathy with independence in political thought, or the Merit System itself, or in new experiments in government which may be of great value if properly pursued.

So, I feel that the tendency is most regrettable for the bar itself, and that if there are some weaknesses in the system of selection by competitive examination and tenure under the Merit System, they are far out-balanced by the very undesirable factors to which I have referred.

➤➤➤➤➤➤➤➤➤➤➤➤◄◄◄◄◄◄◄◄◄◄◄◄

33

Closing Remarks as Toastmaster

(JUNE 1950)

This part of Mr. Seasongood's address at the fiftieth Harvard Class of 1900 reunion dinner at the Boston Harvard Club is reprinted from the pamphlet celebrating that event.

I SHOULD like to add a word in summing up what seems to be the spirit of this occasion. We have an appreciation of those who are gone; we cherish their memory. We anticipate going ahead and doing work and being useful. We don't want to be like that old gent who every morning first thing used to look in the obituary column of the newspaper, and when he didn't see his name there, went back to bed for the remainder of the morning.

That isn't the attitude we should take. I don't think there is any trouble with our own attitude about wanting to go ahead full steam, or even, when necessary, with reduced steam. I have jotted down a few of the incentives and encouragements there may be for you to continue on and see that you can do something, and that there's no reason to stop.

Verdi, for instance, wrote the opera *Othello*, his greatest, when he was seventy-four, and *Falstaff* at eighty. Hobbes, at seventy-six, undertook an analysis of English law, which he did so well that for two centuries he was adversely criticized by the critics. Thomas Hardy, we know, did fine work after seventy. Cheverell, a French chemist, did remarkable work; he got an honorary degree when he was about a hundred, from Harvard. That holds out hope for all of us, if we succeed in living that long. We don't want to be like Francis Bacon, who said: "I do now wax somewhat ancient. One and thirty years is a great deal of sand in the hour glass."

There was Jefferson at seventy-three, who took a forty-mile horseback ride to attend a dinner. Winston Churchill is an inspiration to all. The King of Sweden is ninety-two, and the Harvard Corporation is over 300 and going strong.

I want to call attention to one more thing, the paintings of Grandma Moses Ritalburt. Grandma Moses started painting, I believe, at the age of seventy-seven and is going strong, so strong that all of her pictures command strong, indeed handsome, prices.

I mention those things as an inspiration for you to go and do likewise. Some have this ridiculous idea that when you reach three score and ten, you are apt to be finished. A hundred years ago, a man of seventy was supposed to be dead. Now, he is one of millions that have fifteen years ahead. In fact, old age is that period of life which is fifteen years older than you are. In 1900 the ratio of persons over sixty-five was one to twenty. It is now one to twelve, and in five years it will probably be one to eight.

So, gentlemen, let's go ahead and resolve we will do the best we can, not be daunted by whatever may be approaching problems or obstacles, and "just keep rolling along."

[34]

≫≫≫≫≫≫≪≪≪≪≪≪≪

Third International Congress of
Comparative Law

(AUGUST 5, 1950)

Speaking as the delegate from the Cincinnati Bar Association and the College of the Law University of Cincinnati, Murray Seasongood delivered this closing address in the Old Hall at Lincoln's Inn in London. As such, he also attended similar conventions at Monte Carlo, Monaco, in 1954, and Oslo, Norway, in 1956. Elemér Balogh, termed in this address as the moving spirit of the Congress and of preceding Congresses, is the subject of the speaker's "Elemér Balogh: In Memoriam," in the Tulane Law Review, Vol. 30 (Feb. 1956), p. 315.

WHEN, at the opening session of this Congress, the Lord Chancellor, Viscount Jowett, welcomed the members, he referred to his "predecessor," Francis Bacon. An aphorism of Verulam, that "brightest, wisest, meanest of mankind," is that "an over-speaking judge is no tuneful cymbal." This epigram might, I am aware, be paraphrased and applied, at this late stage of our proceedings, to an overspeaking lawyer. Moreover, some of our sessions were, as you know, held at Kings College; and while I was listening there to an address of length, I was amused to observe, carved into the desk at which I was

89

seated, the plaint of a student: *"Je suis accablé de sommeil."*

It is a privilege to offer thanks on behalf of the American delegates to this meeting. Doubtless this honor comes to me by virtue of seniority, as I am a veteran of the American Bar Association meeting in London in 1924, and of the First and Second International Congresses of Comparative Law at The Hague in 1932 and 1937. I cannot say that any contributions of mine at any of these gatherings have been of an earth shaking character. But I feel sure I have profited by information and, more important, friendly acquaintanceships made and renewed in all of them. When The Right Honorable Lord Reid was giving, this morning, his interesting and informative comments on "The Administration of the Criminal Law in Scotland," he mentioned that free legal aid is furnished to those unable to pay for the services of a defender. This recalled to me that I did introduce, at one of the former sessions, a resolution calling for free legal aid for the poor in both civil and criminal cases. This resolution was approved and referred to the Academy, from the bosom of which it has not been released. But I have long subscribed to the philosophy that "the first thing for the reformer to acquire is a geologic sense of time," and I am not yet ready to go along with Dr. Johnson's "Superfluous lags the veteran on the stage."

Lapse of time has made inevitable that many of the great figures of previous Congresses are not here. I mention with particular affection and sense of loss Dean Wigmore, his modesty, capacity for friendship, vast scholarly knowledge and attainments. We recall him in the terms of the inscription on Wesley's tomb, "God buries his workman but carries on his work."

Our special thanks are extended to those in authority at Lincoln's Inn, Gray's Inn, and Kings College, University of London, who made it possible to hold our sessions within their historic confines. In this beautiful "Old Hall" we think of *Jarndyce v. Jarndyce*, based on chancery procedures that were followed in this very place; and of how it has been possible long since to supplant them with the desiderata of speed, simplicity, and lessened expense that furnish a model for legal systems of other countries.

Finally, any tender of thanks would be totally inadequate that did not include an expression of gratitude to our friend, the inspirer and, more than any other one person, accomplisher of these occasions, Professor Elemér Balogh. Emerson said: "Every institution is the lengthened shadow of a man." To assemble this convocation, Dr. Balogh communicated with 420 persons, including 134 members of universities of 45 nations. He corralled for presentation here 150 general and 228 special reports. His prodigious and indefatigable industry and complete unselfishness and devotion to the great objective of these Congresses are truly beyond all praise. His is a loyalty in the field of international legal understanding, comparison and amelioration, that equals or surpasses the efforts and achievements of Jeremy Bentham and David Dudley Field in the domains of improved legal procedures and codifications. Now that this Congress is ending, he has already begun to plan for a fourth Congress. We say to him, in the words of Horace: "*Serus in caelum redeas.*"

[35]

⋙⋙⋙⋙⋙⋙⋘⋘⋘⋘⋘⋘⋘

The Social Sciences and the Law

(SEPTEMBER 15, 1951)

*During the dedication of the Arthur T. Vanderbilt
Hall as the Law Center of New York University, a
symposium was held on "The Relation between
General Education and Law-School Training in the
Preparation of a Lawyer." At the ceremonies, Mr.
Seasongood received the degree of LL.D. This discussion is reprinted from the New York University
Law Review, Vol. 27, No. 1 (Jan. 1952), pp. 109–11.
Concerning the above subject matter, see Seasongood: "Public Service by Lawyers in Local Government," part of the American Bar Association's "Survey of the Legal Profession," reprinted in the Syracuse Law Review, Vol. 2, No. 2 (Spring 1951), p.
210; also "Should Young Lawyers Be Citizens?" in
the Harvard Law School Record, Vol. 1, No. 9
(Sept. 11, 1946); and "Why a Law Course on Municipal Corporations?" in the Harvard Law Record,
Vol. 28, No. 7 (Mar. 19, 1959), p. 10.*

IT IS REALLY thrilling to participate in this symposium.
I suppose the idea of a commentator is perhaps to be like
the Scottish man who confided he was going down to
the club "to contradict a bit." But I find myself unable
to contradict what has been said. I concur with it in its
entirety. My contribution will be a matter of emphasis.
Senator Fulbright has indicated the importance of the

connection of lawyers with, and the education of lawyers for, participation in the national government. I should like to emphasize local government. While it is often referred to as the lowest, local government is to my mind the highest branch of government in the United States because it is the one nearest to the people and so the one used by them to judge all government. Their confidence or otherwise in government depends on that with which they have come most closely in contact.

We had two lawyers in Cincinnati who were brothers, Charles and Joseph Wilby. Charles was an anti-imperialist. Most of you are too young to remember what a controversy that was after the war with Spain. Joe was more placid and lived longer. He used to say of Charles that if you were to inquire of him "Isn't that a beautiful tree over there?" he would answer "How can you admire that tree when millions of people are in subjection in the Philippines?" I suppose I am a little like that when it comes to being intense on how urgent is good local government. When I go into that subject, I feel that here the lawyer has an important and largely neglected opportunity. I think that the teaching preparatory to and in law schools slights local government. The consequence is that lawyers are missing something of the utmost interest and urgency. It is practically a new subject—all these things have happened in this century: for example only, the council-manager form of government, excess condemnation (not of officials but of property), set-back lines, home rule, zoning and planning, the merit system, freeways, the place of aesthetics, employee unions and the right of public employees to strike, redevelopment projects and public housing. I could cite other interesting advances in local government, but I won't. Disraeli is supposed to have said: "Whenever I want to read a good book I write one." I have mentioned these things in books and articles to which the listener is respectfully referred.

The understanding of experiments and aspirations that have entered into local government is imperfect and not at all clear. How does this situation come about? Well, when the civically untaught get to be judges, they have no appreciation and sympathy for the strivings of local government. It is the stepchild, the ugly duckling, and so it suffers. The important thing I urge is that a law school's teaching should be such as to imbue the student with the worthwhileness of local government, and his obligation to take some part in that field.

The participation of lawyers will help to promote the prestige of the legal profession. De Tocqueville stated over a hundred years ago that the bench and bar were the aristocracy of the United States and that they influenced and molded public opinion. I believe that if we still have this influence and can use it to rid local governments of the mistakes and evils and crudities and wrongdoings that permeate so many of them, and restore them to places of dignity and worth, we shall at the same time do much to improve the position of the lawyer who had a part in bringing about such a great reform.

You have to teach a man who wants to go into local government that he has to be able to stand alone, a very important thing for any lawyer to learn. He must have those qualities which Sir Joshua Reynolds attributed to Burke from lines of Milton:

unmoved . . . his loyalty he kept . . . nor num-
ber nor example with him wrought to swerve from
truth, or change his constant mind, though single.

The person who wants to serve local government must
learn to do that and to stand like Horatius at the bridge.
The young man who realizes the paramount importance
of sound local government and is willing to be its champion must have the courage to do his part regardless of
the drawbacks and sometimes real hardships to himself
that go with such service.

He may lose clients and opportunities for advancement; he may be misinterpreted, defamed, and appear a
failure. But let him learn, on this great occasion, from
what is said here that the goal of achievement of one's
aims is not so important as people think it is, or as is the
consciousness of public duty well performed. That idea
must be impressed upon lawyers. And is not Robert
Louis Stevenson right when he says "To travel hopefully
is a better thing than to arrive" and "The true success is
labor"? Or what William the Silent, the founder of the
Dutch Republic exclaimed: "It is not necessary to hope
in order to undertake, nor to succeed in order to perse-
vere." Or as expressed in Waugh's prize poem, there is a
reward in "High failure towering over low success."

These are the things that the lawyer should learn. Let
him just emulate the great man, Arthur T. Vanderbilt,
for whom this Law Center is named. I think the psalmist
must have had someone like him in mind in the passage:
"He shall be like a tree planted by the rivers of water,
that bringeth forth his fruit in his season; his leaf also

shall not wither; and whatsoever he doeth shall prosper."

As it is, in general, the lawyer wants to get along, to conform, to be on the right side. It is essential that the teaching of law and the preparation for law impress upon him that it is not too important to be on the "right side" nor even to succeed, if his effort in behalf of the local political life of his community has been worthwhile.

I think I have now about said my piece, which is to emphasize that there has been a neglect of local government and local-government law, and that this situation is inexcusable. There are not a third of the law schools, because there are not a third of the bar examiners, that require courses in municipal corporations. If the lawyer is to continue to assume an honored station in society, he must be willing to help in local politics and he must be imbued with the idea of championing sound local government. It is the key to all government, and the excellence of it will assure that the country prosper and that the legal profession will stand proud and erect in cities on a hill.

-»»-»»-»»-»»-»»-»»«««-«««-«««-«««-«««-«««

36

Address of the Day [1]

(OCTOBER 4, 1952)

This speech, made at the dedication of Douglas Putnam Hall, Marietta College, Marietta, Ohio, appears in a printed pamphlet of the event.

I FEEL very happy at being called to participate in today's wonderful ceremony in the life of Marietta, and to be recognized as one of you. I used to tell a story about a supposed Yale man. But because Mr. Putnam attended Yale, I thought I had better change it to Princeton; and then just as I was walking here, Governor White told me that he had gone to Princeton. Now I shall have to change the story to a nameless college. But anyway, this man met another and said: "I'm glad to meet you. I'm glad to know that you went to that college. I'm an *alma mater* of that institution myself."

Well, I can't say that I am exactly an *alma mater* of Marietta College, but I am pleased to be a member of the class of 1950.[2] As you look at me, you might think that I was a bit slow in school and that, as Bob Hope said of his college days, "The years passed, but I did not."

Yet here I am, and very proud to be one of your num-

---

[1] This speech, given from notes, is transcribed here from a tape recording.

[2] The College honored Mr. Seasongood in 1950 with a Doctor of Laws Degree.

ber and allowed to participate in this significant and happy occasion. This dormitory is most appropriately named. You have heard the letter from Douglas Putnam, who is now ninety-one, of Pasadena, California, and the oldest alumnus of the college. As you have also seen from the printed program, he is a member of a family which is distinguished for service to our country, to the state of Ohio, to the city of Marietta, and to Marietta College.

You have also heard here that the years the Putnams were trustees of the college exceed the years of life of the college, because several of them occasionally served at the same time. Douglas Putnam, the grandfather, was born and died in Marietta and, as Mr. Blazier stated, was the first secretary of the board, remaining a trustee for sixty-two years. He was a noble benefactor of the college, giving something over $80,000.

There is an account, with which you are perhaps familiar, how on one occasion when the college was needy—I suppose there are many such occasions, Mr. President, and they still exist; all colleges are needy always—on an occasion when the trustees had expected a substantial contribution, Mr. Putnam came late to the meeting that day, for it had happened that his bucket factory had burned the night before. Nevertheless he came to the meeting and gave $25,000, saying, "Providence has shown me what can become of one's means, and I think I had better give of them before Providence might prevent my doing so."

Douglas' father was David Putnam who came to Marietta in 1798, traversing the wilderness, as has been said, on horseback. He became the first principal of Muskingum Academy, the earliest school of that grade

in the Northwest Territory. Douglas Putnam's grandfather was Colonel Israel Putnam, Jr., a soldier of the
Revolution and in 1788 a pioneer of the Ohio Company
of Marietta. The great grandfather of the elder of the
Douglas Putnams was the redoubtable General Israel
Putnam, senior major general next to Washington of the
Continental Army. He left his plow in the furrow even
without changing his clothes to join the colonial forces
on hearing "the shot heard 'round the world" at "the
rude bridge that arched the flood" at Lexington.

For a story of thrilling adventure it is hard to match
his life. His successful combat with the she-wolf in a
cave, for which he was called "Wolf" Putnam, his resistance to the Stamp Act, his leadership in the battle of
Bunker Hill—or as, I believe, the historians say should
be correctly Breeds Hill—his last-minute rescue from
Indians when tied to the stake and about to be burned,
the wreck of his company and himself off the Cuban
coast in a hurricane—all of these are some of the inci-
dents in that colorful life of the progenitor of the subject
of this talk.

General Rufus Putnam, who headed the founders of
the city of Marietta, was the first cousin once removed of
General "Wolf" Putnam. And I think you will agree that
this Putnam family is of such distinction and achievement as matches the great Adamses or any of the other
great families of American history. It is indeed a proud
thing for Marietta College to know that so much of the
family's interest and effort and help were devoted to the
college. I am sure that Douglas Putnam must have
believed that great ancestory is not merely a matter of
pride, but also an inspiration and obligation to honor

one's forebears by carrying on their tradition of service.

Truly then, to honor Douglas Putnam it is not enough that this building is named Douglas Putnam Hall. Although the name will be thus perpetuated, the influence of Douglas Putnam's personality must enter into those who will dwell in this dormitory. Milton called fame "that last infirmity of noble mind." He may have meant, I think, that perpetuation of a name is not the true essence of earthly immortality.

Consider Thersites and Agamemnon, the one despicable, the other king of the Greeks. Thersites was so malevolent that he said of Agamemnon: "He is a good man and well liked, but he has not so much brain in his head as ear wax." Thersites is a name, Agamemnon is a name; and having been names, they are today nothing but names with no survival of the personalities of these men.

Yet, the good men do enter to some degree in the lives of others. I should say, for example, that the greatest contribution Theodore Roosevelt made was not so much any specific achievement but rather the inspiration and inducement he gave to young men of promise and to forward-looking men of ability and character, to enter into the public service as one of the most noble occupations which can engage the interest and strength of men —and since then, of women, I may add. If the men who inhabit his dormitory now and in the years to come will be inspired by the spirit of Douglas Putnam to greater effort for the public good and to nobler thought, then they will indeed have caused Douglas Putnam to continue to live on earth long after his death.

I should like to suggest some ideas of how you and

those who will follow you in Douglas Putnam Hall may requite Douglas Putnam. I know young people are a little impatient about observations from older people. That's all right. That is one of the mutations of time; and I think that it is all to the good that we elders don't get any preferred treatment for wisdom in what we say merely because of length of years, if there is no thinking behind our words. Polonius was a tiresome old person, although he had many points of good in what he said. Personally, I don't assume any special merit by reason of advanced years.

There is a story of Alcibiades, who was a brash young person, talking with his uncle, Pericles—at least Pericles was related to him—and telling Pericles how Athens should be run. And Pericles, annoyed with his brashness and assertiveness, said: "Alcibiades, when I was your age I talked just the way you are talking." And Alcibiades looked him in the face and rejoined: "How I should like to have known you, Pericles, when you were at your best."

I assume that you will all have a loyalty to the college similar, in some degree, to that possessed by the Douglas Putnams. The inquiry is, how are you to effectuate that loyalty? I suggest first, therefore: resolve to render some public service—particularly some unselfish aid, no matter how small it may seem—to the cause of local government. Local government is still the most important branch of government, closest to the people, most constantly before them, and thus that branch by which they judge all government, either respecting it or not. At this time, when we are so oppressed by communism and the threat of communism, it seems to me one of the best ways of fighting this threat is to solder up the weak places in the armor of democracy. We should not allow government to be a matter of reproach, but make it a thing of worth and dignity so that its worthwhileness provides the best showing of what democracy may accomplish in contrast to other ideals.

Second, think how resourceful were the officers of the college and the successor trustees to Douglas Putnam when in 1945 they purchased a houseboat dormitory to take care of the rush of GI's; and now they have converted this building into a dormitory that can house 270 men and furnish living quarters for them perhaps for a half or a third of the cost of a new building. Our rapidly changing times and insecure world need from such as you ingenuity and alert, receptive minds.

Third, and as a corollary to this, I venture to ask you not to think in terms of maxims, stereotypes, and cliches. There is always an answer to maxims. You can match one against another. It is a lazy man's way of thinking to accept a maxim or a proverb or a tradition without question. It is the lazy man's avoidance of laborious thinking. I remember something I read recently by Lewis Perry, who was for many years the great president of Exeter, the brother of Bliss Perry. He told about school children who were giving pennies. One little girl, when she gave her penny, said: "It is better to give than to receive." The principal said: "Very good." The next little girl said: "Blessed are they that give to the poor." "Excellent!" said the principal. But a little boy who was somewhat grumpy and did not want to give said: "A fool and his money are soon parted."

And so I say, tradition must not be accepted irrebuttably. Tradition is often based on experience and should be given *prima facie* weight. But it should never be regarded as conclusive. Likewise, I call for independence in thinking and action, and not going along with the mob, or even with the majority necessarily. You don't want to be like the politician who, when questioned on an issue said: "I have friends on both sides, and I always believe in being loyal to my friends." Later, it served him right when he asked a woman to vote for him and she said: "You are my second choice." He said: "Who is your first?" She said: "Just anybody."

Sometimes you have to be able to stand alone, or almost alone. That requires the courage of the Putnams. You heard Mr. Blazier tell how the father of General Israel Putnam stood out against the prevalent superstition of witchcraft when it was dangerous to oppose it. Witchcraft wasn't local to this country. The hysteria swept all Europe, as you know if you have ever read Lowell's essay on the subject. Blackstone believed in it. Blackstone said: "Why, of course there are witches because there is a statute against witchcraft, and there wouldn't be a statute if there weren't witches!" And Sir Thomas Browne, the great author of *Urn Burial*, believed firmly in it. And Sir Matthew Hale, a great chief justice of England, believed firmly in it and sent many unfortunate women to their deaths as witches.

Yet the father of Israel Putnam stood out against this prevalent hysteria of 1693 in Salem. He believed that there weren't any witches, and he and a few others held bravely to their opinions. And it was these and England's

Chief Justice Holt who dispelled that hysteria. The accusers of a woman brought before Chief Justice Holt testified that she could fly. So he said: "Go ahead and fly a little for them." Then he directed the jury to acquit that woman. It was solely because people of courage resisted a wrong and wicked prevalent belief that that horrible hysteria was made to fade away and was no longer believed in.

Last, I have the firm conviction that true wisdom and judgment depend largely on character. Of course, there are exceptions. Bacon was the "brightest, wisest, meanest of mankind," and there have been other exceptions. But, in general, if you have a fine character, you think of things without relation to the irrelevant, without personal considerations; and your judgment is apt to be sounder if you have a fine character than if you do not. It is not just an aphorism to say honesty is the best policy. If you can go at things singly with the idea of just determination, and can eliminate all unrelated and personal considerations—well, you have to have a fine character to do that.

I have experienced such situations. I haven't been a judge, but I am on the Loyalty Review Board, which is an appellate procedure—you might say appellate court —and I find how difficult it is, with the best of intentions, to rule out all extraneous considerations and to decide the question on the absolute merits before you and not be influenced by your predilections, wishes, or any personal considerations.

As usual this matter has been best stated in the Bible, in the wonderful passage from the 28th chapter of Job:

But where shall wisdom be found? and where is the place of understanding? Man knoweth not the price thereof; neither is it found in the land of the living. The depth saith, It is not in me: and the sea saith, It is not with me. It cannot be gotten for gold, neither shall silver be weighed for the price thereof. . . .

Whence then cometh wisdom? and where is the place of understanding? . . . God understandeth the way thereof, and he knoweth the place thereof. . . . And unto man he said, Behold, the fear of the LORD, *that is wisdom: and to depart from evil is understanding.*

There are some people, of course, who are ignorant and don't know any better than to stay that way. We used to tell a story in college (if you live long enough, the stories you told come back and are apparently new): two freshmen had been to see a girl, and after they had left, one of them said: "Well, you made a fool of yourself tonight. When she asked if you liked Botticelli, you said that you liked Chianti better. It ain't a wine—it's a cheese."

That's ignorance. But there is also the ignorance of the learned. A person may have learning and know many things and yet be ignorant. And I say for the *summum bonum*, for what we really aspire to—that is to say, wisdom—you must have, in practically all instances, development of character as the basis for it.

I do hope that it will be possible for you to render service in the ways that I have indicated; and if this is done, perhaps you will be able to come to a new appreciation with respect to our beloved College of Marietta, and to think for her in the words of Isaiah:

> *The* LORD *shall guide thee continually, and satisfy thy soul in drought, and make fat thy bones; and thou shalt be like a watered garden, and like a spring of water, whose waters fail not.*

※→≫→≫→≫→≫→≫→≫≪←≪←≪←≪←≪←≪←≪←

37

Bar Surveys of Trial Courts

(DECEMBER 4, 1952)

*This, the second annual Homer S. Cummings lec-
ture on Judicial Administration, was delivered at the
New York University School of Law. Part of the
school's printed pamphlet containing this talk follows. Mr. Seasongood was chairman of the Ohio
Committee, Section of Judicial Administration,
American Bar Association; a member of The Institute of Judicial Administration; and one of a committee of three presenting arguments to the Ohio
Supreme Court for requiring a college degree as a
condition for admission to the bar. See his reviews
of* Traffic Courts, *by George Warren, in* American
Law and Lawyers, *Vol. 5, No. 8 (Feb. 23, 1943), p.
4, reprinted in the* Ohio Law Reporter *(Mar. 22,
1943), and* Model Traffic Ordinance *(Washington:
U.S. Government Printing Office), in the* Journal of
Public Law *(Emory University Law School), Vol. 2,
No. 2 (Fall 1953), p. 431.*

ALMOST EVERYONE who is successful dislikes change or
suggestions of reform which may interfere with his complacency. "New opinions," John Locke observed, "are
always suspected and usually opposed for no other reason
than that they are not already common."

This attitude of those favored by fortune, who least
wish to disturb the existing situation, is not peculiar to

lawyers and judges. In medicine, one recalls the furious attack to which Dr. Oliver Wendell Holmes, father of the late Justice Holmes, was subjected, after he had published in Volume 1 of the *New England Quarterly Journal of Medicine*, his paper on "The Contagion of Puerperal Fever," which insisted that doctors attending women in childbirth were carrying contagion from patient to patient. In our time, the death of Sister Kenny recalls how her new treatment of poliomyelitis was at first maligned by the practitioners as quackery. And just recently in Ohio the State Medical Association opposed the idea of a Constitutional Convention, for fear that if one were held, socialized medicine might be imposed on their profession.

An historic example of hostility to innovation was the conspiracy of the medical and clerical groups when Lady Mary Montague, in 1721, learned at Constantinople of cowpox inoculation and used it on her daughter. Lady Mary had an unfortunate son who caused her no end of trouble, and the Sangrados and predecessors of Dr. Proudie insisted the son's deficiencies were divine punishment for the mother thus seeking to take the issue of life and death out of the hands of the Almighty.

We see the same opposition today to any attempted displacement of the existing order when business is in the ascendancy, and again when labor is in the saddle.

The trouble with lawyers and judges is they revere Eldon and Blackstone and the "perfection of reason" doctrine. Blackstone was hostile to statutes as impinging on the symmetry of the law. He believed in witchcraft, because, he averred, there was a criminal statute aimed at it! He opposed repeal of enactments making capital

160 offenses, many of a trivial character. But Blackstone was a fillip to Bentham, who helped Brougham in his great six-hour speech, in 1828, urging reform of legal procedure. Eldon, too, was a legal high priest of things as they were. Indictments were in Latin until 1730. There was no right of the accused to testify in England until about 1895, and no appeal in criminal cases until 1907.

I am speaking by way of generalization and do not overlook that there have been many worthwhile and courageous efforts by our profession toward amelioration. The lawyers in this city certainly have not sung in unison the lawyer's lullaby "Be still, my child, remain in *statu quo*, while father rocks the cradle to and fro." There often has been much that is admirable in efforts for improvement by members of the bar here. The very great eminence of numerous practitioners, as well as the large number of self-respecting lawyers in this region, have made it easier for some to be independent and outspoken. Then, too, adverse criticism by and of individuals is less direct in a metropolis like this than in the close contacts of smaller communities. One may read with admiration the report of the Criminal Courts Committee in the New York Bar Association Year Book of 1952; the improvement sought in the handling of traffic tickets; the reaction against the sale of judgeships; the efforts to further new and more dignified buildings to house the criminal courts, and much else that is heartening.

Likewise, there have been accomplished improvements in the practice by lawyers in other parts of this country, including my own city and state. Many lawyers and judges have served in the finest traditions of their professions. However, they probably are exceptions; and of others who bring discredit to attorneys generally we are apt to be too tolerant. While some of the brethren have been independent and willing to take chances, it is, nevertheless, one must concede, sometimes risky to seek change, and not all, we sigh, can be flaming archangels. . . .

Bar surveys are good, there are lots of surveys—the question is how are you going to implement their findings? How are you going to give them effect? That is the principal problem once the survey has pointed out possible improvements in the processes of justice. . . .

[After referring to nonaction in Cincinnati, Hamilton County, following a Charles O. Porter report (1947), summarized in the Journal of the American Judicature Society, Vol. 32, No. 1 (June 1948), pp. 1, 14, on the administration of justice there, the speaker continued]:

And now you, I fear, may inquire: "Are dwellers in 'the Queen City of the West' a supine group?" Are they like the prisoner who, when asked: "Do you want to take the stand?" answered: "No, I think I had better remain neutral." No, the majority of our people are not like that. Nor would they take the advice Pickwick vouchsafed in his famous discussion with Snodgrass: "It is always best to do what the mob does." Snodgrass queried: "But, suppose there are two mobs?" Pickwick answered: "Shout with the loudest." Many, however, of our burghers are like that, and there are others who take the bitter advice King Lear gave to Gloucester: "Get thee glass eyes and like a scurvy politician seem to see the things thou dost not." But I do not believe that our people generally are desirous of such things taking place.

Some bar surveys have done a great deal of good and

they will continue to do good, whether all of their recommendations are adopted or appear to be complete
duds. . . .

Pray, do not be discouraged by what I have said. One
has to keep on with these things. They are of value and
will lead to good results. Some years ago I was happy to
represent the judges in a court test of what we call the
"Alley Bill." That is not a derogatory reference. The
"Alley Bill" means that every judge runs in a separate
alley, instead of having a sweepstakes and free-for-all
with everybody whose term expires running against everybody else. By this act, one judge's term will end January
1 and another's January 2 or 3, so that the candidates
stand for election in separate "alleys," and not against
their colleagues. Under this method, the incumbents
run pretty much upon their records. The bill was upheld
by the Ohio Supreme Court. If you are determined to
retain an elective system, such a bill lessens some of the
bad factors that inhere in the ordinary election of judges
in populous centers. . . .

In Cleveland, there is an excellent bar primary far
more effective than any in Cincinnati. There, as with us,
they take a secret poll of the lawyers, on a nonpartisan
basis, but when a judge submits his name to their bar
primary he must promise not to campaign or solicit
funds. The bar does that for him. It must always be
embarrassing for a judge to request campaign funds
and to accept them, or, for a lawyer to face possible dis-
pleasure resulting from refusal to contribute. In those
places where the judge must seek out his funds, the
popular impression is that the large contributors have
special influence if their cases ever come before the judge.

It just is not true! The judges take an oath to support the Constitution, and they have enough conscience, dignity and fortitude to perform their duty fairly and honestly. But impaired confidence in the judicial processes results, nevertheless. Another disappointment is the fact that sometimes our bar will not be courageous enough to support a good candidate for judge irrespective of party. It has happened with us, notwithstanding the results in the bar primary. Yet since it is a secret vote, the lawyers tend to cast it and answer conscientiously, regardless of party label. But then, a certain judge may be overwhelmingly supported in the bar primary on his merits. The opposing candidate may be a numbskull (like one we endured, who said he could not decide an uncontested divorce case until he viewed the premises). Still, if the candidate bears the stamp of the "right" party, those active in the political organization and perhaps officers in the bar association will support the inferior candidate notwithstanding their own, and the adverse opinion of their brethren expressed in the secret bar primary.

Now, of course, what we ought to have is the Missouri Plan, or something on that order, for the selection of judges. Where the ordinary system of appointment prevails, the judges are picked for political reasons more than for merit on the recommendation of the entrenched political leader; and the independents, though they might make the best judges, are completely out of the picture. So, we should continue to make surveys of our problems, organize strength and cohesive action and stir up public opinion. We should believe, as James Russell Lowell declared in a Harvard address:

*New occasions teach new duties, time makes
ancient good uncouth.
They must upward still and onward, who would
keep abreast of truth.*

By keeping the flame of purifying fires alive, much will
be accomplished. One must not fall victim to an attitude
of cynicism or despair. The obstacles are great, but can,
and must, be overcome.

Further surveys would show, I am confident, there
are many modern instrumentalities that can be utilized
to make law less expensive, more expeditious, and more
responsive to the will of the people. There is also a
selfish interest involved in improving the administration
of justice; because, unless lawyers do something to remove delays, expense, and uncertainties, court procedures
will be abandoned in favor of administrative tribunals.
In some instances these uncertainties and inequities have
been allowed to continue, until finally potential litigants
have become impatient and said: "Let's get through
with this thing, we can't bother with it." For example,
instead of stenographic reports (where political official
stenographers are often not too good and their transcripts
not accurate), you could utilize the modern instrumen-
tality of tape recording; microfilming could be employed
to save space and time and effect economies for the
government in keeping records; you could use photostatic
processes. Now while I suppose photostats are fairly well
recognized here, there are other media with which you
can accomplish much by utilizing modern instrumentalities. With us, I remember that a good many at our

bar made loud outcries when photostating was sought to be introduced for recording deeds. The objectors appeared to be very impartial about it. They pleaded the cause of reaction with the dignity of a judge. Actually, what they did not want to happen was that persons who had political appointments for copying and comparing deeds for recording—persons who were supposed to typewrite them, but who could not typewrite without making a batch of mistakes—would, because the positions would be abolished, be let out.

There was one huge fellow engaged in this recording. He had to sit way back from his desk. (Maybe I am not slender enough to be talking about *that*.) But this typist's deeds were full of mistakes. Not only that, his pounding of the typewriter punched holes in the paper. When the reform recorder asked: "Where did you get your training for this job?" out came the reply: "I was a blacksmith." Yet, when we tried to get this photostatic process adopted, there were many lawyers who said that the photostats were not indestructible; that they were not legal; that they were hard on the eyes. They gave a million reasons for why they did not want the process to be brought about—all except the real reason. Now this reform has been established, and everyone is pleased with it. You get exact, permanent, immediate copies of your deeds and papers without any trouble.

It is not only in such fields and with trial courts, though, that reforms can be implemented. Our Federal Court of Appeals for the Sixth Circuit has just adopted the rule, used in the Fourth, Seventh, and perhaps other Circuits, of not having to print the record on appeal. Printing costs for appeals have become staggering. Now, also, in cases where printing is required, there are courts allowing use of offset printing to diminish expense.

If the personnel of the lower courts were appointed under the Merit System, there would result greater efficiency, a greater dignity and a better observance of the law. As it is, however, political appointees employed in many courts are concerned with dealing out favors. They intercede to fix traffic tags, fail to stamp on traffic tickets the fact of prior convictions, and generally ignore their primary functions. One of our objectives should be the installation of a system assuring adequate career service and dignified court personnel, removing their jobs from the reach of political favoritism.

Under present conditions one may very well inquire whether the grand jury has outlived its usefulness. In a number of places, as in England, it is regarded as unnecessary, unduly expensive, and outmoded. When grand juries are under political influence, they hand down or withhold indictments according to the wishes of the prosecutor. As an example, there was a rather gross election fraud perpetrated in Cincinnati recently. One of the offenders was arrested for voting under another's name, but when his case was presented to the grand jury, the matter was ignored. . . .

Another improvement would be to make the time of attendance of parties and witnesses more convenient. As it is, a number of cases may be set for nine or ten o'clock, and then delayed for hours. The litigants and witnesses sit around, waste their time, and become resentful of the processes of justice. Soon you hear comments such as: "I had better stay out of this thing" and "I don't want to have anything to do with this." There used to be a time when oculists made people wait before getting to see them, so as to impress upon patients how busy the eye men were. I can remember when there would be an entire room filled with people, while they waited to enter, bathing their eyes with cotton dipped in water from bowls. Although there was no sense to this, it was customary. Oculists are more considerate now; and with like consideration by judges, a staggering of cases could be arranged in which suitors and witnesses would be called for particular times. By approximation, even if there were occasional breakdowns in the calendar, these would be inconsequential in comparison with the greater convenience of litigants and witnesses and the acquiescence in court procedures that would result.

There is also an acute problem inherent in punishment, readjustment after release and possible regeneration. I feel we have failed almost completely in these fields. The problem of divorce also needs attention. I should say one-half to four-fifths of the daily filings in Hamilton County are divorce proceedings. Although I do not know how general this ratio is, I imagine a somewhat similar percentage prevails elsewhere. Considering the very great number of these divorce cases, the possibility exists not all of them are completely veracious and honorable. In England a judge of probate, divorce, and admiralty, asked what he did, replied: "I deal with collisions at sea and collusions on land." Instead of just running these filings through the grist mill, we should make a more thorough study of their genuineness and of the causes of divorce and get to the root of the trouble.

There is much that can be done to improve some of the doctrines as well as the functioning of the law. For example, take our old friend "contributory negligence." I used to make a living out of contributory negligence, assumption of risk, and the fellow servant rule. Now that I am more "mature" and can consider these things in a fairly aloof manner, contributory negligence altogether defeating recovery seems a faulty doctrine. No matter how slight the lack of due care, so long as it contributes directly to the injury, all recovery is prevented. The admiralty rule of division and the comparative negligence law in some of the states and statutes are much more equitable. As another doctrine requiring re-examination, joint tort-feasors generally cannot have contribution, although there is no particular justification for that rule. All such anachronisms and warts on the law ought to be eradicated.

Part of these purprestures on the road to legal progress are procedural and part are substantive, but together they present a challenge. We must remove these in order to make the profession to which we have devoted our lives one of dignity and honor; to establish a legal tradition of service, which it must be, for the preservation of our institutions. What ought we do? What is the answer? It is very simple. Someone said of Mr. Churchill—his needs were very few; all he wanted was the best of everything. And all I wish is a simple formula that will ensure a new and improved sense of public morality. Without it, bar surveys and attempted reforms, although not useless, will be evanescent in their consequences.

It is the students, neophytes in the law, who must help develop and firmly build this sense of public morality. Ultimate success is not indispensable. There is a real delight in going ahead with a good cause, irrespective of how incomplete the victory or how small the success that attends your effort. As Emerson said, in ringing words: "Who so would be a man must be a non-conformist." That is, for us, he must not accept legal defects silently. Valuable, too, is Bryce's observation: "The chief duty of the good citizen is to be angry when anger is called for"; and G. B. Shaw wrote well: "The reformer is one who will not take evil good naturedly." Let us lawyers save ourselves from complacency! Truly, as said in Proverbs, "The righteous man falleth seven times but riseth again."

>>>->>>->>>->>>->>>->>>->>>-((<-((<-((<-((<-((<-((<

38

Fifty-one Years of It

(JANUARY 17, 1955)

Transcribed from a stenographic report is this ad-
dress delivered by Mr. Seasongood before the Day-
ton, Ohio, Bar Association. With a most active
private practice of the law, he also managed to de-
vote valuable time to many public and semi-public
legal appointments and employments. Among these
were: special counsel for Cincinnati in its gas-rate
controversy before the Ohio Supreme Court and
Public Utilities Commission, 1932–4 (Seasongood:
"Those Old Age Rate Cases," Public Utilities Fort-
nightly, Vol. 15, No. 12 [June 6, 1935], p. 702); spe-
cial counsel for the Hamilton County Board of Edu-
cation, 1953–5; representing the Hamilton County
common-pleas judges in the Ohio Supreme Court to
sustain the validity of the "Alley Bill"; representing
a lawyer charged with contempt of court for advice
given (article: "The Lawyer and Contempt of
Court," Bill of Rights Review, Vol. II, No. 2 (Win-
ter 1942); counsel for the Cincinnati Teachers As-
sociation; representing the County Charter Commis-
sion, of which he was a member; giving informal
legal assistance on the constitutionality and func-
tioning of the Ohio Turnpike Commission while he
was a member; vice-president and counsel of the
Cincinnati Smoke Abatement League.

IT IS ALWAYS a pleasure to come back to Dayton. I have
had associations with your bar for a great many years

and have enjoyed them and I congratulate you on the excellent work that your Bar Association does.

Somebody (Congressman Jeffrey, I hope you won't feel offended) said the Congressional Record was not printed for profit and is read the same way. That may have reference, too, to what I have to say and you to hear. This is not a bread and butter talk, and these are the reminiscences of a person who has been at law for a very long time. Mr. Iddings mentioned that we came to the bar in the same year, and I am glad to see him chipper and lively. At that time you had to wait around in Columbus until you knew whether you had passed the bar examination; and, not having anything better to do, we went to the penitentiary—as visitors—and if I live to be a million, I shall never forget the horror of that experience. So many evil persons confined within that space and, to my mind, so little hope for regeneration according to the archaic system of punishment under which we operated and still operate. That is one of the things in which we have to make more substantial progress than we have evolved in the last fifty years. You know about the lawyer whose client said "They are going to electrocute me tomorrow morning, what shall I do?" The lawyer counseled: "Don't sit down." I remember they had a trusty who showed us about and took us to the electric chair and let us sit in it. Then they showed us, for purchase, a souvenir photo card of the chair and on the back of it a picture of the condemned who had sat in it, never to rise again, with a brief history of the crime of each.

As one gets along in years, he finds you just keep

going, and are glad to keep going, and the way to do it is to go on and not stop.

I was up here, some of you may recall, on the occasion of the recent dinner for Judge Nevin and wanted to tell a story, but the shortness of time prevented. I was told that I could have five minutes. I wanted to tell about how I happened to get a new tuxedo for the occasion and so was reminded of my dear friend, Isaac Mayer, now about ninety years old, of the distinguished Chicago firm of Mayer, Meyer, Austrian, and Platt, and he came down one night at the hotel where we were staying, in a magnificent new tuxedo with wine-colored lapels. I said: "Old boy, you must have gotten a ten-dollar fee or something," and he said: "Hush, don't tell anybody, but I ordered this to show my gifts are not in contemplation of death."

I was telling some of the fellows before lunch about a dear friend in Cincinnati, a very distinguished Dr. Zenner, who is a lifetime friend of our family and is now 102 years old. A year ago he bought safety razor A instead of razor B because the latter was guaranteed only for three years while A was guaranteed for life.

The first case I had in the District Court in Cincinnati, in the Southern District Court of Ohio, was in association with that very great leader of your bar, Honorable John A. McMahon. He and Mr. Warrington, later Judge Warrington, with whom I started, worked on a great many cases together, and it was a privilege to be associated with those two very grand personalities. This was in some aspects a rather amusing case.

You had here the Dayton Computing Scale Company,

which manufactured a barrel-shaped scale—a great advance in the art. It had numbers and could compute prices with great accuracy. Orange O. Ozias was president. I don't know whether Mr. Ozias of your bar is a descendant of his or not. They had an enterprising salesman who got out a "Dear Madam" circular, as he called it. It read: "Dear Madam: Can you do this on your scale? Buy 9 pounds of pork roast, sell it at cost, and make 5%?" The competitor was a Toledo computing-scale company represented by a man named Theobald who got his training (I hope I am not hurting anybody's feelings) in the early days of the Cash Register Company when their methods were not too precise and they had a good deal of freedom of action. He called the circular "a shameless admission," and distributed it by the thousands so labeled. He would go in and buy up an old scale and break it up with a crowbar and get a brass band and say to the crowd: "Here is this crooked scale and the shameless admission that shows they are cheating." They were not cheating at all. It was a little catch way of advertising, because you would sell it and profit legitimately on the half cent. If it was nine cents, you would cut it in half and charge four and a half cents, and the custom of the trade is that the half-cent or over is kept by the seller, and that was the answer to the whole problem. Nevertheless, it got to be a serious matter, because Theobald was flooding all the places where this scale existed with these signs. The question was whether an injunction could be obtained, and I was allowed to argue the application for the preliminary injunction. Of course, the rule is you cannot enjoin a libel, but you can enjoin a conspiracy. If the libel is part of a conspiracy, you can enjoin the libel as part of the conspiracy. Judge Thompson (I was a pretty young fellow then, it was in 1906) listened with an intent expression. He was a grand old man and a solid judge. (Of course, you always think that of a judge who decides in your favor.) He granted the preliminary injunction under *Emack v. Kane*, 34 Fed., and that line of cases, which held to the effect that I have said.

Incidentally, we once had a lawyer at our bar whose methods were not always above reproach. I should say he was the Cincinnati variety of Howe & Hummel in New York, and he fooled around with a U.S. grand jury. He represented some bucket-shop operators who were being investigated, and Judge Thompson had him up for contempt. The Cincinnati *Enquirer* printed a misprint too good to have been accidental, in which they said: "Mr. —— indignantly claimed in his own defense that he had been practicing 'low' in Cincinnati for thirty years."

Well, the Toledo company was represented by Clarence Brown of Toledo, a tremendously able, attractive, cheeky lawyer. He was a real person. I liked him very much. If you remember, he left a great fortune. He represented and invested in Libbey Owens Glass and all that in early times, and I think about every lawyer in Toledo and way points was involved in the will interpretation suit of who were to get the charities he provided for in his very large will. Well, in his appeal of the *Scale* case, instead of arguing the legal point on the preliminary injunction, he set out to show that the scale was in fact crooked; that it just wasn't an innocent thing; they were just seeing who could cheat with this scale. His clients got some trickily weighted packages, and he went before the Court of Appeals, with an old scale, the only time I ever saw a complete deviation from the record, and they were all tremendously interested. Judge Severance was a tall man about six feet two or three; Judge, later Justice, Lurton was a short man; and Judge Richards, the third judge, was nearsighted. One of them looked down on the scale demonstrated and played with it in the afternoon; one looked up at the scale; and the other could not see the scale, and their opinion said, as it appeared to them it *was* a crooked scale. Well, hell broke loose then with the scale said to have been condemned by the Court of Appeals for the Sixth Circuit. We met for conference, and Mr. McMahon said: "Let's file a supplemental bill." It was on appeal from the preliminary injunction, and Mr. Warrington asked of Mr. Ozias: "We can show damage, can't we, from this?" And Mr. Ozias (he was a stout man like I am) started to wriggle around and wasn't very convincing that we could show damage. In fact, it appeared as if many butchers liked it, if it was a crooked scale and the company were selling more than they had ever sold. So Mr. Warrington said: "Hadn't we better get some more evidence before we file a supplemental bill?" Mr. McMahon said: "John, you remind me of a client I had in Dayton who rushed in to me one morning and said: 'Here is a piece in the paper about me which says I, in a night gown, jumped out of a first story window and was pursued by an irate husband flourishing a revolver. Can I sue them for libel?' I answered: 'That depends on whether it was true or not.' He scratched his head and said: 'Hadn't we better get more evidence?' "

Eventually the computing-scale company came out all right; but it was a long struggle, and I have taken too long telling of it, except that it has relation to the very great man at your bar with whom, as I said, it was a delight to work.

Mr. Warrington, of whom I still think with gratitude and emotion, was a most able, profound, and terrific worker. He started in at once in the morning and would go all day without lunch. I was a young man then with a good appetite (half of which is still true), and he had an old stenographer who was almost deaf, and who would sit there smoking a stinking stogy. When the boss dictated, he did so loudly and very slowly, and John Meeker, the stenographer, would turn over his notebook and write across it: "Juicy roast beef, rare, baked potato" and show it to me while he was waiting for the next dictation and I for something to eat. One night we worked until about seven o'clock and took one of the cable cars they had then, up the hill and we passed the Schneider catsup factory on Sycamore Street. Mr. Warrington said: "My, that smells good. That reminds me, we haven't had any lunch." I said: "I knew it all the time." He was a most indefatigable researcher and would get immersed in his work and continue it at home at night and as soon as he came dashing in early in the morning. One day he swept in and did not notice there was a new office boy, and he said: "Call Kenan." Kenan was President of the Gas Company. We represented that company in those days. Kenan was a tough old bird. Of him and his company, a part of the verse was: "He wore a white beard, did Norman Kenan, when I last seen him."

.   .   .

Incidentally, he was in politics a good deal, causing a rather amusing citizenship incident. An Italian was up for naturalization, and Judge Hollister asked him: "Do you belong to any political society inimical to the government?"

The applicant said, smiling: "Yes, Judge, your honor— Yes, Judge, your honor."

The judge got apoplectic and the veins stood out. He fairly shouted: "You tell this court you belong to a society hostile to government, a political society?"

"Yes, Judge, your honor—yes, Judge, your honor."

"What is this subversive society you belong to?"

"The Norman G. Kenan Republican Club." He was telling the truth and didn't know it.

Well, this office boy called Kenan, and Kenan did not seem to know what the deuce Mr. Warrington was talking about. They were supposed to be discussing a franchise, and finally Mr. Warrington got very irascible and exclaimed: "What the blankety blank! Who is this?" The answer: "I'm Jim Kenan." Jim Kenan had been a former catcher of the Cincinnati Baseball Club with Tony Mullane as the pitcher. He had been a saloonkeeper and, I believe, a councilman. . . . The sole Kenan this boy knew was his hero, of the great battery, Jim Kenan, and Mr. Warrington said such awful words, the little fellow got down on his knees and crossed himself in the outer office.

Now, old Mr. Tom Paxton, the other senior partner, was a lovable man, too, and a wonderful business getter, who had every kind of person you could imagine as a client, and all had faith in him. He was of solid judgment and fine character. He told me that in the early days the

Cincinnati team had Tony Mullane (you are all too young to remember Tony Mullane), a great pitcher with a black handle-bar mustache, and a sturdy fellow who pitched two games in succession, when they used to have five balls and four strikes, and you could foul as much as you wanted, and the catcher would not come up behind the bat until very nearly when the count was critical, because, with insufficient protection, he was apt to be hurt. Well, Tony Mullane jumped his contract and was going with the St. Louis team and we were hired by the local club to enjoin him, under *Lumly v. Gye* and *Lumly v. Wagner:* you can't, by court order, make an opera singer sing for you; but if he is an opera singer of great value and experience, you can enjoin him from singing for anybody else; and the client wanted to enjoin unique Tony from pitching for anybody else. Mr. Paxton told me that at that time they had old U.S. Judge Baxter, a big-jowled, able but arbitrary tremendous fellow from Tennessee. This was in the early nineties, and the firm's young man came back trembling like a leaf. He said: "The judge is going to put me in court for contempt." "Boy, what have you done?" and he said: "I stated the case and Judge Baxter said 'I am going to put you in contempt for bringing a prize fighting case into my court.' " He did not know anything about baseball and thought that it was something related to prize fighting. Well, I won't devote any more time to that to tell you how it came out, although it would be rather amusing.

I had an interesting baseball case once in which I represented the Chicago Club. Their gate receipts were tied up at the opening game, and I removed the case to the Federal Court. It must have been about 1919, after

Judge Peck had been on the bench only a short time. It was the Lee Magee case. Magee was sold by Cincinnati to Chicago, and Chicago discovered that, as they thought, he had played crooked ball when he was with Cincinnati and they let him out. He contended first that he had not played crooked ball on the Cincinnati team; and then he said that if he had, it was in a former employment and there was no showing that he had not played perfectly correct ball for Chicago, and Chicago had no right to let him out for possible peculations in a previous employment. Do you wish to guess how you would have decided that? I found a case in Texas that said if the retention of the employee with knowledge of a defalcation in a previous hiring would injuriously affect the relation of the employer and his customers, then the employer had the right to let him out. That issue was submitted to the jury, and they found against Magee. The National League used to give me a lovely baseball pass to all the fields for a good many years, but I never used it, so it lapsed.

Mr. Paxton was a great raconteur. He was speaking once about his old friend, Judge Bradley. There was a case in the Ohio Supreme Court which was 60 Ohio State 309, involving gambling (a very interesting case: I advise you to glance at it), and Bradley's opinion said: "These people played a game which the record showed was known as poker and instead of using money, they used some celluloid little disks of varied colors which represented different values, and the record shows these were known as chips." Everything he said was supported by "The record shows this, and the record shows this," never indicating he knew anything except from the record. Mr.

Paxton said: "The damned old hypocrite, I played poker with him many a time."

I had a very interesting contract case, *McKell v. the Chesapeake & Ohio Railway Company*, which was tried three times. Governor Harmon was governor at the time and came down and, as I think perhaps inappropriately, tried it to a jury for the railroad. The first time we got a directed verdict against us; the second time we got a verdict for $300,000, and they had a record which showed I had said to Judge Hollister: "I don't think you should direct a verdict in our favor. I think it would be error if you did." But he did anyway. That was reversed. The last time we got $125,000, and that stuck. Meanwhile they had tried certiorari to the Supreme Court twice unsuccessfully.

In that litigation I was associated with the late Judge John H. Holt of Huntington, West Virginia. He was one of the finest lawyers I ever knew; one of the loveliest, bland characters, no resentments or animosities toward anybody. He was a great trial lawyer and a great personage, but he had a weakness for looking on the wine when it was red, or any other color. It was hard on me, as he liked to drink champagne cocktails, and I don't like to do that in the middle of the day. But I had to go along with him and kind of teeter totter into the court room. They told a story about him when employed in a case in the highest court in West Virginia (the judges knew him and knew his weakness). He went on a terrific toot the night before and to bed with his clothes on, and a colleague pulled him out of bed in the morning, unkempt, unwashed, his eyes red, and rushed him over to court who were sitting there waiting for him. He started in, "Your honors, I am sorry to be late. I have been having trouble with my eyes. I stopped at the oculist this morning and you know how they are, he kept me longer than he should have and that's why I'm late." The Chief Justice asked: "What was the name of your doctor, Judge Holt?" Answer: "Dr. Williams." "Well," the Chief said, "that's strange, I was with him at eight o'clock last night when he died." I asked my friend: "What did you do?" "What could I do?" he replied. "I went ahead and argued the case."

I had another interesting association with Judge Holt, in *Main Island Creek Coal Company v. the Cleveland and Western Coal Company*, tried to U.S. Judge Westenhaver, and a jury in the Northern District, and I had an experience there which was most unusual. There was a woman on the jury panel, a fine-looking woman—I mean she looked like a person of substance and independence— and I asked her questions, the answers to which showed she was qualified, and nothing that she was not. Her husband sold his entire output to one customer, a street railroad company. Well, they had nothing to do with the case, so I let her sit. There followed a despicable trick; the president of the defendant got the president of the street railway company to come and sit with him at the table and appear to confer with him, apparently assisting in the defense and in every way indicating he was a friend and wanted him to prevail. I did not know whether that was a contempt, and if so, not to pay any attention to it; so I figured if she was the right kind of woman she would be more resolute than ever, and if she were not, there was nothing you could do. She went right through with it and joined the rest of them, and we got a verdict for $404,000. She told me afterward: "I knew what they were doing and if that was going to jeopardize my husband's business with that company as a customer, I couldn't help it. I took my oath and I stood by it."

I had a case for the *Davison Sulphur Company v. the Cienfuegos R. R. & Power Company* of Cuba involving some pyrites that were not shipped, and in that case we got a verdict in the Common Pleas Court of $805,000. The man who brought me that case was, I think, the secretary of the American Bar Association at the time, and no sooner had the verdict been rendered than he said: "What are you going to charge?" I answered: "Well, my golly, I have been so busy with the case I have not been thinking of what I was going to charge." He said: "I want to know what you are going to charge. I am taking the train right away and I want to know your charge." I said: "What's the hurry?" And he said: "I find gratitude is a short lived emotion and I believe in letting a client have it right away. They like it better, they do better for you, and they have a greater appreciation of what you did than if you let it lag, and it is my habit to send in a bill right away." I think the advice was probably of more value than the amount of judgment we got which was largely uncollectible.

I was called in once for a man named Harrison, charged with using the mails to defraud; he had some kind of bath tubs that were supposed to be fraudlent bath tubs. I forget whether they burbled or what was the wickedness of the bath tubs, but the prosecution were bringing witnesses from all over the United States against this poor fellow, and his lawyers were so busy defending him that they could not reach a question that arose when, right in the midst of the trial, the postmaster did one of the most contemptible things I ever saw officialdom do. He issued a fraud order against this man and gave it wide publicity; and defendant counsel hired me to see whether that could be enjoined. I stayed down Saturday and Sunday and knocked out a bill of complaint, and at that time in *McNulty v. the Magnetic Healing* case, somewhere around U.S. 177 or 185, it was decided that although the postmaster has absolute discretion in such matters, when it is such a clear abuse of discretion as not really to amount to an exercise of discretion, it is enjoinable although it is said by the terms of the statute that his action is final. I went in to Judge Hollister with my bill the first thing on Monday morning, and he said: "I agree with you, this thing is an outrage," and he called the local postmaster up without considering whether he had to join the postmaster general, which worried me a good deal, and said: "Well, you just don't put that fraud order into effect. You are enjoined from doing it." So I came out and told them what had happened, and they said I was a fine young man, and I went around patting myself on the chest. I was so sorry for the accused, I did not think to send him a bill. He was convicted and became bankrupt. It did not matter that the conviction was reversed in the upper court. Judge Hollister was very susceptible to any suggestion of fraud, and this case was reversed for some such reason in the upper court. Meanwhile, as he had become bankrupt, I never got a fee. And my advice to you young fellows here is, get your bills in early and don't wait because sorry and sympathetic.

I had a collie case once where a witness was a dog. It

was a question of disputed ownership. To use a collie as a witness was a little risky. It is a somewhat fickle dog; you cannot always rely on it. But this collie was all right. When it came to our man and he was in the courtroom, the dog got up on his hind legs and fawned on him, petted him, licked him, and pawed him affectionately, and all that. When the other claimant was there, the dog slunk away from him. He was about the most magnificent witness, human or otherwise, I had ever had. They sued us, and we counterclaimed, and the jury was so mad that they granted in our favor the whole of our counterclaim.

As to these experiences, of course times were different. I think the sociability of the bar and the traditions of the bar are worth a great deal, and it is a pity if we have to lose them under changed conditions and lessened litigation under which we operate. I used to be in court much of the time, for a great many years. The litigated practice now has fallen off somewhat. There is a variety of new things in modern law. We used to use English cases; they are all out. The rule of precedent is greatly lessened, *stare decisis* is much less than it was. . . . And I think that with the growth of Administrative Law, none of which existed early in the century, when ordinary litigations were just tort and contracts and a few statutes, the whole practice of law is changed. In the old days Motion Day was on Saturday, and we would all go up and chat around and get acquainted with one another and, while waiting, have a pretty nice time, except when your motion was not granted. It was very pleasant to be in association with the bar that way.

I remember once Judge Spiegel, on the bench, had to hear a motion on a question of damages which they were arguing. I was sitting in the jury box waiting for my motion to come up, and he was puzzled and said out loud: "What is the name of my friend in Memphis?" I jumped up and interjected, as self-appointed *amicus curiae:* "Hadley v. Baxendale, 9 Exch. 341?" "That's it," he said, "his name is Hadley." And so helped him remember the name of the case he wanted to rely on—his friend lived in Memphis.

Well, lawyering has been a happy time for me. It has gone by very quickly. . . . I find it a delightful profession. I would not do anything else for the world. I never knew what a calm and peaceful profession it was until I got into politics, where there is no covenant of quiet enjoyment; although I also have the feeling that out of our busy lives, and for the honor of our profession, we should devote some attention to public affairs and to aiding, to the extent we can, in the operations of the government. I think it is very urgent in these times particularly, when we are under attack from communism and you have a great many super 113% patriots who inveigh against communism and yet are willing to have evil conditions in political government exist, and particularly in local government; thus giving the best argument to the Communist, as showing breakdowns in the democratic processes. I feel it is a high obligation of every lawyer to take some part toward betterment of conditions politically and otherwise in his local community.

Dryden said: "Not even heaven itself over the past has power. What has been, has been, and I have had my hour." Maybe you think I have had more than an hour. I have enjoyed chatting with you and appreciate having been invited to be your guest.

234

Anniversary of U.S. District Court,

Southern District of Ohio

(FEBRUARY 10, 1955)

This address in celebration of the court's one-hun-
dredth anniversary is transcribed from a stenographic
report of the proceedings. Mr. Seasongood had ad-
dressed the Annual Circuit Conference of Federal
Judges for the Sixth Judicial Circuit, at Cincinnati,
June 7, 1947, on "The Judge from a Lawyer's View-
point." From 1941 to 1944 he was a member of the
Advisory Committee on Rules of Criminal Proced-
ure, appointed by the U.S. Supreme Court. A report
concerning these rules in the making appears in his
address before the Missouri Bar Association at Co-
lumbia, Missouri, Sept. 24-6, 1942, printed in the
Missouri Bar Journal, Vol. 13, No. 8 (Oct. 1942),
p. 163, and also in the Missouri Bar Journal, Vol. 13,
No. 9 (Nov. 1942), p. 215.

MR. PRESIDENT, your Honors seated on the Bench, other
Judges who are here, friends of the District Court and
hardy survivors, including myself as the puisne. Please to
spell that correctly, Mr. Reporter. It is p-u-i-s-n-e. Please,
not puny.

I do not know but what I may have been introduced
before this morning when his Honor, Judge Druffel, said
that later there would be some old relics on exhibition in

the courtroom. I wish, though, to reserve an exception, your Honor, to the remarks of the last speaker saying our course is nearly run. So far as I am concerned, I am just beginning to run.

I notice on the program it says that immediately after I end, Court will be closed. So I think I should speed along, and, to add a touch of the classic, quote from Pliny, the Younger, in his first book of Epistles: *"Nihil Aeque in Causis Agendis ut brevitas placet."* Former President Angell of Yale once said of my Latin, I talked it like a graduate of the Sheffield Scientific School. Anyway, to translate: "Nothing pleases so much as brevity." Or, to paraphrase for this occasion: "Just because the Court has been able to continue for a long time, is no reason why the speaker should do the same."

I was happy to hear the Judges and Mr. Justice Reed, who spoke, emphasize the importance of this Court. We all know, as Mr. Justice Holmes pointed out in a famous decision (*Towne v. Eisner*, 246 U.S. 418), that a word does not always mean the same thing. I never had the slightest doubt that when the Constitution, Article III, Section 1, referred to the Supreme Court and the "inferior courts," the words meant merely courts of original jurisdiction or of appellate intermediate jurisdiction, with the Supreme Court in contradistinction; and not at all that the District Court was not comparable in importance and dignity with the other courts to which its decisions might go.

It is a privilege to be a part of an enduring institution. We, our work and efforts as individuals disappear; but there is a continuity about an institution, which renders labor for this court agreeable and satisfying in the thought that our strivings make its traditions and precedents and perpetuate its accomplishments, even after we are no longer able to serve as its officers.

To employ a simile that may be understood, especially by Mr. Justice Reed and others from across the river, we lawyers are, you might say, the char of the barrel which gives the contents its color. I shall not press the simile further. I do not wish to be branded as an "Old-Fashioned."

As has been said, the District Court has gone on and will go on. It has occasionally met with oppositions and resistances and attempts to curtail its jurisdiction and limit its importance—I mean, not especially this Court, but all United States District Courts.

I refer particularly to some of the statutes that have been passed, under the reserved power of the Congress to do pretty much what it wants with respect to the District Court. Thus, it has been prevented from restraining collection of a tax of a state where a plain and efficient remedy is there available in its courts. It has been prohibited from enjoining proceedings in the state courts, except under very exceptional circumstances.

The Court's power to remand to the state courts has been made absolute, because there is no review from an order of remand, by error or mandamus or any other way; and the decision to remand a case to the state court appears to be final and unreviewable.

Likewise, a state statute may not be invalidated here, except in certain instances, and usually by a three-judge court.

And I should say these restrictions are all fairly advisable, to prevent a conflict or causing it to appear, that the District Court is really something apart from the court of the state in which it sits.

The most serious threat, of course, has been the Norris-LaGuardia Act of 1932, limiting the power of the Federal Courts in labor controversies, to issue restraining orders and injunctions and to punish for contempt.

Now I think that *Erie Railroad v. Tompkins*, 304 U.S. 64, decided in 1938, and overruling, after ninety-six years, *Swift v. Tyson*, 16 Peters 1, has been a kind of boon to the continued existence of the Federal Courts.

I was a sufferer from *Wabash Railroad v. Adelbert College* in 208 U.S. 30, where the Supreme Court of Ohio, in *Compton v. Railway Co.*, 49 O.S. 592 (1888), decided one way that some unsecured obligations of a constituent railroad had become secured by consolidation; and the Supreme Court of the United States decided exactly the opposite in *Wabash Railroad v. Ham*, 114 U.S. 587, on the same obligations, with the result that those not drawn into the Federal Court got about a million dollars and our clients got nothing, and I very little.

So, I didn't have too much liking for *Swift v. Tyson*; and I was glad when *Erie Railroad v. Tompkins* came along and the Federal District Courts were assimilated so far as questions of general law were concerned to the state courts. And I believe that that will mean, as time goes on, much less resistance to the jurisdiction and powers and procedures of the Federal Court than if it still remained a court concerning which you queried: "Where should we bring or remove this case? Will the law be better for us in the Federal Court than in the State Court?

Because of the Erie Railroad decision of the Supreme Court, I see little reason why this Court should not go on, from strength to strength throughout the years, served by competent and honorable judges and by an assiduous and high-minded bar; and so there may be upheld in its confines our ancient maxim: *"Fiat justitia ruat caelum."*

The Independent in Local Politics

(NOVEMBER 19, 1955)

Murray Seasongood's address, transcribed from a stenographic report, was delivered as part of a Conference of the Citizenship Clearing House for Western Pennsylvania at and directed by the University of Pittsburgh. The title of the address, given in Webster Hall, was under that part of the program entitled "The Impact of National Parties and Issues on State and Local Politics," and expressed "The Non-Partisan View."

Concerning this subject matter see Seasongood: "George Washington and Political Parties," in The American Scholar, *Vol. 1, No. 3 (May 1932), p. 265; also "How Political Gangs Work," in the* Harvard Graduate Magazine *(Mar. 1930), p. 261, reprinted in the Cambridge* Tribune *(Sept. 13, 1930), p. 12.*

WHEN YOU TALK about the party system and adherence to it, the first question is: "What do you mean by a party system?" In Burke's definition, a party is "A group of persons associated to advance common principles in which they all believe."

In our American party system an inordinate part of its activities is devoted, crudely stated, to "Who gets what and how"; or, as Ambrose Bierce puts it, "The conduct of public affairs for private advantage." In no other country, I believe, where the two-party system is conducted is so large a portion of the work of the party devoted to demands of patronage, giving special favors and putting the "deserving," that is, political workers, into positions, often without respect to the merit system or without other qualification than vote-getting ability. You cannot talk in generalities. As I see it, you have to talk of the political parties as they are conducted in this country.

I found observations last night of Dr. Seyler, Deputy Secretary, Department of Internal Affairs, Commonwealth of Pennsylvania, most interesting, including that local political organizations must be nourished and maintained in order that they co-operate with the national and state governments in projects that originate in those termed "higher echelons."

True, when we speak of the tiers of government (and it could be spelled two ways), municipal government is the lowest. But it is such only as a foundation is the lowest; because it is the most vital; and the safety of the republic rests more on good local government than it does even on state and national government. It is becoming more and more pervasive, and is that government with which the people have the closest contact. And, accordingly, as they respect it and believe in it, they believe in their country and its traditions; and to the extent that they become cynical and indifferent and despise the way it is conducted, they become less attached to the principles of all government of which it is so vital a part.

I told Dr. Seyler, informally in discussion, that I differ with his thesis that you have to have an alliance or concatenation of the local and state with the nationally instituted program. I consider that that is the very worst thing you can do. You must have a contact with them, and co-operation with them. But it should be based solely on the merits of the proposition; and the responsible head of the local government—mayor, city manager, or whoever he is —should be the representative to speak in terms of merit and not on the basis of political strength. Because if you do go into that, then you get very bad results in the development of the national program.

Dr. Seyler humorously referred to Mr. Dooley and his animadversion on reformers in general. I don't know how many of you recognized the allusion when I said of Mr. Dooley that his view was colored because of acquaintance with Bath House John and Hinky Dink in Chicago. Bath House John was a rubber in a massage, or Turkish bath, and got to be the corrupt boss of Chicago politics for many years. Hinky Dink, his collaborator, was the little saloonkeeper who blew so much foam off beer that when he died, he was worth a million dollars. It takes a lot of beer to do that!

Lords of the Levee is a book that describes the depravity in the great metropolis of Chicago in those days, with Yerkes, the utility magnate, co-operating to bring about a degradation that would have made Caligula or any of the other old professional bad men of history blush. The depth of shamefulness in our second greatest city under those conditions was unfathomed and menacing to the Republic. That is what you get with a good many of these local gangs. Winston Churchill said of Bevan: "He always has his feet firmly planted in the clouds." That is what people like to say about the reformer: that he is visionary. And of a mugwump, you know their definitions: "One who has his mug on one side of the fence and his wump on the other." All those jocular references

to reformers are just not so. Reformers have as much political and other sense as anybody else, and sometimes a
good deal more, and the professional politician is not the
wizard he is reputed to be, so that often the Independent
will have good breaks and get somewhere by reason of
foolish mistakes of the professionals.

Now, what I am trying to say is that cities co-operating
politically and not on the merit of a proposition with the
national organizations is a serious mistake. In Cincinnati, William Howard Taft proclaimed it when he was
Republican Secretary of War and as a famous Akron
speech about forty-five years ago. In it he advised people
to vote for the Republican state ticket, headed by Myron
Herrick for Governor, but to vote against the local political machine in Cincinnati and Hamilton County, and he
mentioned the great fortunes that some of its bosses like
George B. Cox, August Hermann, and Rud K. Hynicka
had accumulated without any visible means of how those
fortunes were gotten, and, therefore, it was not ridiculous
to suppose they had gotten them by the illicit means of
their political power.

If you are going to have your local affairs administered
through the federal government on a basis of party affilia-
tion, you get some very bad results. You may say I am
going back to old times. But the same bad practices persist. Thus, rather recently, I jousted with one of the old
bosses, Fred Schneller, now deceased. (I was fond of him
in a personal way, and he liked me. He would have cut
my throat in a political matter, but he would not have
taken pleasure doing it. There are some others who
would, like the man who, asked if he was going to a certain funeral, answered: "No, but I approve of it.")

This last campaign I had an anonymous postcard from a fellow. He wrote: "Paxton (my firm is Paxton & Seasongood) is dead; Seasongood will be shortly," and signed it "George," and I said on the radio later that I didn't know who George was, but I inferred he might be a descendant of George B. Cox, whose wife had borne him no children.

Well, those are little knock-down pleasantries that you undergo in a long career, and you get kind of used to giving and receiving them. As after a steamer went down, a woman said to another: "How terrible that all those passengers were lost." The other inquired: "What about the crew?" "Oh," said the first, "they are used to it." So you do get kind of used to it, and after a while you don't mind those things and take them in good temper and get along somehow.

To come back to local affairs: I was talking about Schneller, who was in council with me in the first administration. He had been there a long time and lived in a quiet, simple kind of way. His estate, the size of which had not been disclosed when they went through the state office of inheritance tax, was finally fixed for federal estate tax at about $1,000,000; and that may have been small. Just recently, as I came up here on the plane, I read in the Cincinnati *Enquirer* about a man I had referred to, in one of my radio addresses, as a fence for a burglar. I got by with that. I was not arrested or sued for libel, slander, or anything else, because I knew what I was saying and was fortified by conclusive evidence when I said it. He was ward chairman of the Republican organization of the 16th Ward, and he just recently had been assessed by the government on back income tax of $239,000 in four years.

Now such are the people often influential in your local political machine. And I may mention the bad effect of the local political machine's influence on the national parties. For instance, Cincinnati is overwhelmingly Republican and has been for many years. I am a Republican. I am much more a Republican than a lot of these fellows who asseverate they are Republicans. I was one of the original "Ike" men around Cincinnati, and that was not easy to be, I assure you, with the organization solid for Robert Taft. What I am saying is that while I am a regular Republican in national affairs and have always voted for presidents and senators who were Republicans, sometimes it gave me a headache to do it. There are a lot of our local dominant machine who are not ardent Republicans, but use the label of Republican, and I assure you their organization is much more vitally interested in electing a treasurer, sheriff, coroner, and other county officers than for the election of a President of the United States, and their controlled voters are overwhelmingly herded for the candidates of their local crowd more than for President of the United States. In the case of Ike, I don't think there is any doubt they dragged their feet and went along very unwillingly, as they had done on previous occasions for other Republican candidates who did not, they feared, completely talk their language.

I shall give you instances of where it was wrong to have the local political approach to a national problem. Cincinnati is, as I say, overwhelmingly Republican. So, when it came to the selection of a place for the Regional

Reserve Bank, it was planted, through the influence of Newton D. Baker and the Democratic party in power, in Cleveland, rather than in Cincinnati, where it belonged geographically and sensibly because it serves a locality of which Cincinnati is the center. That was a case where local political influence dominated the nation and produced a bad result in the spending of the national funds. Likewise, in locating our airport, "Dear Alben" Barkley, who is pretty influential, as you know, as the Veep and otherwise, caused our airport to be taken away from Cincinnati and moved across the river to Boone County, Kentucky, where we have to wind through the city of Covington and its inadequate streets to get there, with a great waste of time and loss of prestige to the City of Cincinnati.

And the same is true of other things I could mention and keep what I am saying nonpartisan. It does not matter whether those called Republicans or Democrats happen to be in power nationally, the principle is actually the same. They believe that the local Independent is an Ishmael and a pariah; and he has not a look-in with the national government, and is penalized for doing things that are for the betterment of his local community. That is the way these political organizations work.

When the former city boss of Toledo was postmaster general, and Cincinnati was going to have a new post office, there had been selected a site in which a number of local Republican politicans and "best citizen" supporters were heavily interested, and they were going to sell that to the national government at an exorbitant price. I (I hate to say I. I do not care whether it was X or I) helped prevent that, by pointing out the absurdity and outrageous consequences of putting the Federal building where they planned to have it. They want perquisites and also patronage, and patronage demands are all they are after, and they exert their influence on the national government to reward them for money payments and the efforts they have made supposedly in behalf of the national government. And they are the only media of communication, and citizens have to deal through them when they want this and they want that in the state or national government.

And just recently, when it came to the selection of a judge: We have a very eminent Court of Appeals for the Sixth Circuit which embraces Michigan, Ohio, Kentucky, and Tennessee, and I have a special veneration for it because my first boss, the late John W. Warrington, in 1909 became a judge on that Court. The late Chief Justice William H. Taft started as a Federal judge there, and Judges Day and Lurton of that court became Justices Day and Lurton. It is truly a distinguished court. There was a vacancy, and the Republican machine of Cincinnati put forward a candidate they got Senators Robert Taft and Bricker steamed up to approve, telling the latter I was against their pet man. They were intent on getting this person appointed as a matter of patronage, and X went and made an issue of the advisability of that selection, which was finally withdrawn.

Now I mention those instances, of which many could be given, where co-operation between the local and the national on the basis of low political desire and advantage is a distinct detriment to operations of the national government.

I believe the Independent can do much more good by

nonaffiliation in local government with either of the two national parties. I base that on experience. I became a member of the Republican Executive Committee in 1912 to 1915, after it was declared they were to reform from within and had leading citizens of Cincinnati, largely successful industrialists of very prominent connections, agree to serve, supposedly to reform from within. Well, without going into the details of that experience, I found that these magnates were imbued with the idea that the world would end if it were not for the machine. They were unlike Emerson, who, when a Seventh Day Adventist told him the world was coming to an end, replied serenely: "That's all right, we can get along very well without it." They definitely believed that the world could not get along if the Republican party were not maintained in all its strength down to and into the gutters; and so the local organization must be allowed to flower and develop. Perhaps not flower, but grow. Still, flowers can grow from certain kinds of fertilizer. Anyway, their idea was that you must allow these local organizations to have their own way and do whatever they want, to keep up the strength of the Republican national political organization. So, I pulled out.

I mention now what the Independent can do. Cincinnati's regeneration started in 1923, in a purely accidental way, when I made an inflammatory speech in a little association we called the Cincinnatus Association, composed of about fifty, mostly rather prominent young Republicans. We regularly discussed local affairs, and in my speech I said that our government was at stake. We had a council of twenty-six from wards and six at large. Why they were permitted to be at large nobody ever discovered. There was a Democrat in once, and they bowled him over legally some way, so it was unanimous and all were dummies. Many were saloonkeepers. Now, I do not have anything against such, but I do not favor having a council almost entirely composed of them. It is said that on one occasion someone dashed into a council meeting and shouted "Your saloon is on fire," and they all ran out. But, anyway, the thing was that Cincinnati was called the worst governed city in the United States. In that opening foray against an extra tax levy, everybody was against me: all the papers, all the wise people, all my friends (your friends are generally against you), and they said: "You are trying to sabotage the operation of the government." The *Times Star* editorial (that is the Taft paper) said I was a Bolshevik, which was the bad word of that day, about the worst they could call you. I said: "Don't give them any funds. What you need is a new council-manager government, a small council elected at large, possibly with proportional representation" (which I now believe was the salvation of our government in Cincinnati). And that was the origin of the whole thing. It went on.

Here was a miracle that survived over thirty years with the opposition against it of the regular official local Republican organization which dominates the county and Cincinnati (abetted by two of the three newspapers) and where the Democratic organization is so weak and inconsequential that it takes the crumbs from the winner and in many instances co-operates with the dominant organization.

The Independent has raised Cincinnati to the pinnacle on which it stands and has maintained it there under handicaps that seem almost insuperable and almost un-believable, to achieve and hold what has been done. That accomplishment is by Independent movements, pure and simple, and therefore I have reason to believe that that is what you can do as an Independent in local affairs; and that there is no reason at all why the national parties, for their own good, should have local leeches hang on to them in the interest of patronage, favoritism, and low ambitions and activities.

The first thing an Independent should know is how to fail in good humor. There is always a residuum of ac-complishment if you have enough tenacity to hang on. You are going to accomplish something even if there is an apparent failure. To my mind, the method to bring results is for the Independent in local affairs to vote for his own sake, for his own community's sake, and for the sake of the national parties to rid them of this bad old man of the sea who rides on them and demands patron-age and low performance in the local subdivision or thence to national government.

The fight never ends, ladies and gentlemen. You might think, with Cincinnati's achievement, persons of means and influence would be convinced it has been extremely good for them in a financial way. But they are not. They want to stick with the Republican organization and they will stick with it, no matter what it does or what is shown against it.

I suppose what motivates them is that they want to have, through approachable and "reasonable" bosses, an "in" to the state government and they want to have an "in" with the national government, so they can get to talk impressively to both about things that concern them.

Because if you were to put adherence to the machine on any basis of economy or common sense, there would be no justification for maintaining an organization so discredited and disreputable as this organization which has existed for so many years in Cincinnati.

This last campaign was a honey. I just could wow you with it. But my wife is going to give me fits for all I said here today. I have talked out freely here; I may not do so at home. She says: "If you are going to use those adjectives, go into the bathroom, shut the door and use them, I don't care to hear them." Anyway, I shall boast a little about this last month's campaign, which I think was the most active I was ever in. It really resolved itself into five different campaigns; one of which was the re-election of the Charter councilmen, and at this time may I show you how important every vote is. The last person was elected by a majority of 100 votes in a 150,000 counted vote (more than that, I guess), now being contested. I don't know what the outcome of that will be. Then there was an effort to kill proportional representation. They hate P.R. since they can't get control of the city under it and because it assures a critical minority if they should get control. And so, for various pretexts, they have been fighting P.R.; and at this time they also submitted a voting machine bond issue to put voting machines in Cincinnati which could not count the P.R. vote, and therefore they would be prepared to say: "Here you have invested five million dollars and you can't have this silly system here which prevents your using the machines in city elections every two years. So, get rid of the P.R system." I felt I had to go out and make a fight on that, and I printed a letter in our three papers as a paid, full-page advertisement. With others I talked around, yelled, and waved my arms. The vote was overwhelming against the machines. Finally there was a Citizen School Committee that endeavored to get qualified persons on the school board irrespective of their political belief.

But this organization will not let anything alone. They won't let the office of judge alone (a nonpartisan office); they won't let the schools alone; they won't tolerate honest voting and counting of ballots. They are voracious. They are intent on getting everything into their maw and swallowing up everything where there is possibility of patronage, sabotaged Merit System, and favoritism.

Somebody said: "As you get warmed up, your audience gets warmed down." I suppose you are sufficiently cooled down by this time, so I'll quit.

Jamestown, N.Y.

(NOVEMBER 1956)

*This speech was tape-recorded by Mr. Seasongood
in Cincinnati, transmitted to Jamestown, N.Y., and
broadcast there a number of times in the successful
campaign to retain Jamestown's nonpartisan system
of electing council.*

IT IS A PLEASURE to recall my visit to Jamestown and
speaking there on city government a good many years
ago when, I believe, your grand old mayor emeritus, Samuel A. Carlson, was mayor. I feel honored to have been
asked to express my views now of the proposed charter
change from the present nonpartisan system of election
to bringing about party primaries and partisan elections
in your city affairs. Based on my study and our Cincinnati
experience, I am of opinion that the proposed change
would be unfortunate indeed, and that for the best interests of Jamestown the suggested change should be dis-
approved by the voters. Students and writers on the
subject of municipal government are almost unanimous
in deploring election on national party issues of municipal officers. The cities are of enough importance to have
real issues relating to their own local problems. As the
business of a city expands, with new services constantly
required, and the problems of limited revenues, the gov-

ernment of a city becomes more a business matter to be conducted as closely as may be in the way successful businesses are conducted.

Moreover, in your community, I understand, Republicans outnumber Democrats two to one. So, you could not well have a two-party system any more than that system obtains in the South and elsewhere where one party so predominates. It then becomes a one-party system with the minority practically disfranchised. I am and always have been a Republican in national affairs; but in our nonpartisan Cincinnati government, those like me and I do not hesitate to vote for the best man. And, since 1925, when we changed from political primary and partisan elections to nonpartisan petition nomination and election, we have had, on the whole, excellent city government which has persisted. In the county, where partisan political primaries and election are held, the government is poor and wasteful, showing none of the efficiency that characterizes the city administration. It is my opinion that you, too, have had good government in Jamestown ever since 1925. Why then should you depart from what has been proved through a generation to be good?

The idea that a city can get more if its city government is of the same political opinion as that of the state or national government is unsound in principle, and, even if treated as so, is subject to the possibility that the state and national governments might be of opposite politics from the city government. State and national matters should be decided on their merits and not by the injection of any political influence. Again, you do have under your present charter two dominant parties: Greater

Jamestown and the Progressive parties. I judge that each of these parties is recruited largely from persons having the same ideas as to their party platform respecting municipal issues.

Almost everywhere now municipal elections are in the odd-numbered, and state and national in the even-numbered years. This is a recognition that local and national issues should be kept separate and better consideration of each is thus obtained. Your political situation seems to parallel Cincinnati so closely that I hope the two, having prospered over about the same period with nonpartisan citizen government in local affairs, will continue to do so as a guide and inspiration for other communities.

-»»-»»-»»-»»-»»-»»«««-«««-«««-«««-«««-«««-

42

Recollections of a Founder

(JANUARY 26, 1957)

Murray Seasongood's address at the fiftieth annual
meeting of the University Club in Cincinnati is re-
printed from the Bulletin of the Historical and
Philosophical Society of Ohio, Vol. xv, No. 4, p. 311.

A SMALL BOY was brought by his lawyer father into a
court room where sat three robed justices, listening perhaps, with eyes closed, immovable, while the lawyers
droned on. Suddenly a fly alighted on the forehead of
the majestic, domed, bald head of one of the justices;
when he brushed it off, the boy exclaimed in excitement:
"Look, Papa, one of them's alive"! We mature charter
members are gratified to be termed "active" on the program and "founders" rather than "foundered." Also, we
are pleased with the solicitude shown by the board for
our welfare, including their offer of transportation to and
from the club. Doubtless they have ambulances, or worse,
waiting, in case of emergency, to cart away any of us
needing such conveyances.

I have been asked to say something of the early history
of the club. In Thornton Wilder's *Life in the Sun*,
Admetus, Alcestis, Apollo, and Hercules (those first two
named are hard to utter after all the wine you have served
us) are principal characters. Hercules is a stupid,

drunken, lecherous, athletic-scholarship type of boob. A maiden (perhaps that is not the right word) says to him: "Hercules, tell us how you killed the Hydra." He replies, scratching his head: "It wasn't easy."

Now, I don't really go back so far as Hercules, and have not, I hope, his unpleasant characteristics. But I can use his words "It wasn't easy" appropriately with respect to the beginnings of the club. This was true for a number of reasons: to start safely, we felt that we needed 200 members. Candidates having the necessary means and qualifications were not readily obtainable. A requirement for membership was at least two years as an undergraduate in a college, or a degree from a professional school. While we were considering and obtaining candidates, a rival group was started by persons who were not eligible by these standards, and some others, for membership in a university club. They hurt us considerably by soliciting prospects and attempting to negotiate for the property being contemplated by us for use as our clubhouse. There was a feeling among members of the board that it would be best to take in this rival group as a whole and thus get rid of their interference. Mr. Joseph Wilby, first vice-president, and I were obdurate (the only time I have been that way either before or since), because believing if we were to be a university club we should be just that or the name would be a *lucus a non lucendo*. We finally had our way (again, the only time that has ever happened to me), and this possibly competitive group then failed to eventuate and fizzled out.

Another acute problem was where to locate. There was a rather general feeling that the city was moving to

the north, away from Fourth Street, and the region of
Fourth and Broadway was not the Picadilly section (I
mean that pleasantly) that it has since become. The
club district could be said to be in the neighborhood of
Eighth Street. Thus, the Literary Club was then on the
south side of Eighth Street, east of Vine, next to the red
brick building where Thomas Buchanan Read, a member
of that club, wrote *Sheridan's Ride* in 1864. About opposite was the Blaine Club building, which, believe it or
not, had been owned by some of my family, and whence
issued at intervals serried ranks of political stalwarts
crowned with white beaver hats and also wearing "the
white flower of a blameless life." The Woman's City
Club was housed in the former quarters of the Lincoln
Club, a somewhat more fashionable Republican Club, at
the southwest corner of Eighth and Race. The Queen
City Club was at Seventh and Elm, and the then recently
built, impressive Phoenix Club was on Race Street between Eighth and Ninth.

There was a strong sentiment for my maternal grandfather's house, built by him some fifty years before, on
the north side of Garfield Place between Race and Vine,
where now much foam is blown from beer by members
of the Cuvier Press Club. I therefore left to the other
two members of the committee charged with obtaining a
site the final selection, and I have always been happy
that our present house was obtained. It was a small
place (there were those who loved it), at once homey
and dignified. We did not have the ladies' side on Broadway we now enjoy, and the east extension on Fourth
Street did not come until about 1920. In the Seely home,
there were fine woodwork, book cases, mantels, large mir-

rors, and a magnificent heavy wallpaper in the front hall and up the stairs, of dark background with embossed figures in gilt onlays. It was a matter of regret when, some years ago, this fine wall covering was removed. The addition we now use of a substantial hand rail on the front-stairs balustrade as a safeguard for the bibulous or decrepit is poor compensation for this sacrifice to modernity. The three members of the Executive Committee had the job to furnish and equip the club. This was a considerable undertaking, what with lambrequins, drapes, linens, china, cutlery, pots and pans, stoves, glass, carpets, oilcloths, and the numerous other supplies required to launch the enterprise. There were endless discussions and bids and, for me, education for a later marital state.

Altogether, the life of the club was, for the first several years, tenuous. Three persons, especially, helped save it: Harry Mackoy, Ed Ernst, and Schmick. Harry was one of the finest men I ever knew, a lovely character, always most considerate, conscientious, and painstaking. Ed Ernst, our first president, who remained in the office for many years, "had a talent for friendship." He was aided by his father-in-law, Frank J. Jones, a major of the Civil War and a very grand old gentleman. Ed, Harry, and others helping made new members feel at home, introducing them around, particularly to the large and varied group that frequented the well-attended and interesting Round Table. They saw to it that no one ever left the club after a visit feeling he was unwelcome or should not come back regularly. Irwin Schmick (I think Irwin was his first name, but no one ever called him anything but Schmick) was a veritable Phileas Fogg's Passepartout. There was nothing he could or would not undertake, except to say

259

yes. He always said no, but would set out to do just what was asked and more. We were holding on rather precariously; so he would, when occasion demanded, help wait on table, cook, scrub or paint floors, hang pictures, and at a time when liquor was hard to obtain, surreptitiously provide it. He married and lived in the club, and little Schmick was born and grew up there, until he was helped by some of the members to go to Kenyon College. Schmick had been found by Al Morrill, a member of the Executive Committee, at the old Burnet House, in a rather subordinate position. He brought with him some of the Negro waiters there and so established the practice, which has prevailed ever since, of having them as our dining-room servitors. They have performed, almost without exception, with great fidelity and competence, many for long periods of time. One of the first was Andrew Johnson, who had nine children. Each played a different musical instrument and yet managed to preserve harmony in his home.

Many of our board members helped to make the club enjoyable and keep it going. We used to have very good stunts put on by members of the club. Mr. Waite, here, reminded me of a lark the late Henry Hunt engineered about 1913 while mayor. He caused some of the board members to be arrested and taken by police officers to the nearby police station on Broadway, for giving an entertainment without a license. Mr. Waite represented the accused and, of course, they were triumphantly acquitted and released. The regular dinners of the Board of Governors were lavish and agreeable affairs, made possible by somewhat heavy fines of governors not attending meetings.

Now that the club is an established Cincinnati institution, it is somewhat difficult to think of its having had an early period of stress and uncertainty of life. Its objects have, I think, been measurably attained. That is as much as any human being or institution ought to expect. Twenty-five years ago I expressed the view that there should be occasional talks or discussions that could easily be had from some of many learned or distinguished persons visiting the city. I repeat that suggestion now, because no one, I am sure, remembers what I may have said twenty-five years or twenty-five seconds ago—and that is all that saves me. If our purpose were stated to maintain friendship among "educated college men," that would be better than, as now expressed, "among college men." The two are not necessarily the same. The only truly educated man is he who continues his education for his whole life, not merely one who goes to college. As a somewhat sardonic critic observed, Thomas Gray wrote a great poem ending "Where ignorance is bliss, 'tis folly to be wise," and added, the title of that masterpiece is "Ode on a distant prospect of Eton College."

In conclusion, may I venture to hope that after your hearing these fugitive recollections and comments, you may find apposite the description of the Peasant by the Wanderer in Wordsworth's "Excursion":

A man he seems of cheerful yesterdays and confident tomorrows.

➤➤➤-➤➤➤-➤➤➤-➤➤➤-➤➤➤-➤➤➤◄◄◄-◄◄◄-◄◄◄-◄◄◄-◄◄◄-◄◄◄

43

A Birthday Message

(OCTOBER 24, 1958)

The rabbis, officers, and trustees of Rockdale Avenue Temple arranged a special public service in honor of Murray Seasongood on the occasion of his eightieth birthday. On this day Mr. Seasongood received a warm commendatory letter from President Eisenhower.

How CAN I sufficiently thank you for making this service possible, for the laudatory testimonial, illuminated and framed, read and presented to me by you, Mr. President, and for the kind expressions accompanying it. I am sure I do not deserve this honor and should liken myself to a spavined, sway-backed old nag entered by its owner in a fancy horse show; not, he said, with the idea of winning a prize, but because his pet animal would thus be in such very good company. Dr. Reichert has mentioned the Talmud, that "you are not to praise a man to his face more than half his worth." Those who have so generously favored me tonight with this service and citation must have done so realizing that the Talmud is advisory only, and that it does not have the authority of Scripture. For, the testimonial given me is not one-half, but many times the extent of recognition I could possibly merit.

Still, I cannot say I am not pleased that they exceeded the Talmudic fraction of permissible praise. It may unnerve me a bit; but I suppose I can stand it every eighty years. Especially gratifying is that the kind words have been said while I can hear them.

A part of Psalm 90 is:

> *The days of our years are three score and ten, and if by reason of strength they be four score years, yet is their strength, labor and sorrow.*

or, as sometimes expressed:

> *Yet is their pride, but travail and vanity; . . .*

I do not take either of these doleful conclusions too literally. Unlike the intense seventeenth-century religionist Voetius, who asseverated that there is not a word contained in the Holy Scriptures which is not in the strictest sense inspired, the very punctuation not excepted, I feel rather, about fourscore years, the way a fellow octogenarian put it:

> *Youth was a vale of doubt and hesitation*
> *Now memory gilds it with a magic touch.*
> *Old age was horrid in anticipation*
> *But since it has come, I like it very much.*

Besides, there are other Biblical passages I prefer to this portion of Psalm 90. For instance, there is Genesis, Chapter 4, Verse 3, in which the Lord vouchsafes to man that his days shall be 120 years. That really gives something to aim at and a basis for resolve, the best thing to put aside for old age is the thought of it. Also, the truth is that a very great number of years of life here is, on the whole, not too important, if one goes along with

William James: "The great use of life is to spend it for something that outlasts you."

I am devoted to our temple. For one reason, because it is so much older than I am, and there are not too many persons or organizations now in that category. My great uncle, Jacob Seasongood, was president more than a hundred years ago and helped bring to it, as rabbi, the great reformer David Lilienthal. My own contacts with this venerable institution have stretched over two thirds of its existence, and with this edifice since the cornerstone was laid by my uncle, Lewis Seasongood, then president, in April 1905. More than seventy years back, while I attended Sunday School in the basement of our old Mound Street temple, my father, on the Sunday School Committee, with other members, made weekly visits to the classes. I remember the impressive red beard, fine presence, and smooth utterances, with an Australian accent, of Dr. Benjamin, the rabbi; the devotional chanting of the splendid musician and deeply religious cantor, Chasan Goldstein. Mr. Kronacker, the president, was a tall, rugged figure when, with peremptory "Pennies please," he garnered from the boys and girls alms for the poor. We had dignified and distinguished teachers, one of these the young and handsome rabbi, later Dr. Philipson, always throughout his long service to the congregation especially understanding and lovely with children.

I hope you will not consider me a boastful ancient if I mention having received the Fox silver medal (for what, I forget), several books as prizes, and that at confirmation I said the confession. Much later I taught an advanced Sunday School class, using as textbook Dr. Philipson's

The Jew in English Literature. And I have had other contacts with the temple, some of which I am glad— for "The old order changeth, yielding place to new; and God fulfills Himself in many ways"—are being carried on by another generation, which includes our daughter, who lighted the candles at this service, our son-in-law, a Board member; and also our grandchildren are here. So, receiving tonight a tribute from this temple is the more precious coming, as it were, from a lifelong and cherished friend.

Ecclesiastes admonishes:

> *Let thy words be few.*

Perhaps my interpretation of this has already been too latitudinarian. So I conclude with Wordsworth's couplet:

> *Enough, if something from our hands have power*
> *To live, and act, and serve the future hour.*

⋙⋙⋙⋙⋙⋙⋘⋘⋘⋘⋘⋘⋘

44

Testimonial

(MAY 12, 1959)

Shortly before the close of the last lecture by Murray Seasongood at the University of Cincinnati Law School, at which he had been a part-time professor over a thirty-four year period, to his surprise the door suddenly opened and Dean Barrow, the faculty, and the entire student body filed into the classroom, some carrying the gift of a huge, beautifully ornamented birthday cake on which were thirty-four lighted candles. All remained standing while Dean Barrow and the president of the student body made complimentary addresses, to which the recipient replied. Later, a "Tribute to the Honorable Murray Seasongood" appeared in the University of Cincinnati Law Review, *Vol. 28, No. 3 (Summmer 1959), p. 269, written by the editors and board of the review. In the* Cincinnati Alumnus, *Vol. 34, No. 1 (Oct. 1959), pp. 5–8, is an article by Mr. Seasongood entitled: "Confessions of a Teacher," which comments on his law teaching.*

WELL, this is hard to take. I have become callous to occasional "slings and arrows" of not too "outrageous fortune." But a mark of esteem such as you have just given me is not easy to receive without display of undue emotion, and makes me wonder how I had enough breath left to blow out the candles. Perhaps you are like the congregant asking her employer for her wages in advance, so that she could contribute to their preacher who was leaving, and to whom they wanted to give "a little momentum."

More than once Dean Barrow has been good enough to request me, even after I passed threescore and ten, to continue teaching. Now, however, like St. Denis, I carry my head under my arm and have become professor emeritus. As a friend, who may have been slightly mixed in his understanding of that title, said: "Fine! They ought to have given it to you long ago." Last week, there was a pleasant easing-out dinner tendered by the university governing body for the emeritus professors, each of whom received a suitably inscribed silver salver on which, if so minded, he could conveniently carry his head.

Teaching law for more than a generation has been one of my most pleasurable experiences. It makes me concur in the statement that "the best way to learn is to teach"; and, as Erasmus said, "The glory of the instructor is in the success of his pupils." The law relating to local governments, always fascinating, has changed and developed in the past half-century, so that it is virtually a new subject; and especially now needs to be done over wisely and devotedly to fit the many mutations brought about by new conceptions and experiments, from altered methods of transportation, new and expanded services required, and use of new instrumentalities. All these have caused a metamorphosis from traditional municipal boundaries, under rigid state laws, to what may be suitable for modern conditions in terms of metropolitan regions under home rule and how such shall be administered. These changes in the municipal law field are somewhat comparable in interest and importance to those that followed long ago in other exciting areas and eras.

After all these years, I am still occasionally stumped for a reply to a keen pupil's question or reasoning. And I can echo, at mature age, Michelangelo's *"Ancora Imparo,"* comforted to recall that he was nearly ninety when he said that; and I am only eighty!

None but proud and brave souls, of whom I am not one, can be indifferent alike to praise or blame. The recollection of this occasion and your kindness will always bring to me a glow of pride, appreciation, and happiness.

Good Neighbor Award

(MAY 22, 1959)

Murray Seasongood received this award at the Isaac M. Wise Temple during the "Good Neighbor Sabbath Service" of the congregation.

CICERO quotes Naevius as having said that "he rejoiced not so much at being praised as at being praised by a praiseworthy man." Rabbi Wohl is such a one, and it is especially pleasing to receive this award from his hand. He is of the opinion that good deeds, in any field, are a part of true religion. The 200th anniversary of the birth of Robert Burns is being observed this year. While I am sure Rabbi Wohl does not approve of all that Burns said and did, I am equally sure he agrees with Burns's

> *The heart's aye that pairt aye*
> *That makes us richt or wrang.*

It is gratifying not only to be presented with this award by one for whom I have such high regard, but also by him for an institution, the Wise temple, to which I feel so closely drawn. Dr. Johnson said that what is nearest touches us most. But I am, I fear, sometimes a Seventh Day Absentist from another temple, although I was confirmed there at the corner of Eighth and Mound streets, and for some time was a member of its Board. I like to

recall that more than a hundred years ago my grandfather, Marcus Fechheimer, was president of this congregation. In 1854 he was active in bringing to Temple
K.K.B.Y. from Albany Dr. Isaac M. Wise, who became
its great rabbi. My grandfather loyally supported Dr.
Wise in modernizing the congregation's services and ritual
and his pioneering on behalf of Reform Judaism in the
United States. My mother, as a young woman, sang in
the choir. I always feel a spiritual warmth when I enter
the lovely old synagogue at Eighth and Plum streets.
Now Rabbis Wohl and Goldman are following in the
path of Dr. Wise. They are again modernizing the conception of religion, this time to embrace a practice of
recognizing those, irrespective of sect, who have made
efforts for the good of the community. These rabbis
dedicate a Sabbath each year to the cause of "The Good
Neighbor."

I am proud, also, to become one of such a group of
those, for each of whom I have great admiration, who
have previously received the Good Neighbor Award.
One of them especially, Al Segal, has been to me a *fidus
Achates*. . . . Moreover, it is pleasing indeed for me to
receive an award for participation in local affairs, because
my belief is that to strive to better these and local political life and to serve the many is, for the citizen, among
the greatest of peacetime, patriotic duties. I suppose I
may be like a long-time resident of Boston who was
thought would be consoled by a Job's friend on not having become a member of the Harvard Corporation, a
position to which he had aspired. The comforter said:
"But just think of the national honor you recently got,
being made first assistant to the secretary of the Treas-

ury." "Yes," replied the recipient dolefully, "but that was only national."

I hope also I do not resemble the disagreeable person who, after having spoken slightingly of someone, had cited to him: "Thou shalt love thy neighbor as thyself" in Leviticus, and responded: "I am not so stuck on myself, either." The many kindnesses, of which this is the culmination, I have been receiving recently, make me tend to believe I must be thought, by some of those who have been so generous, not to be in the excellent health I seem to enjoy, but to have pretty much arrived at the Delectable Mountains from which can be seen the Celestial City. However, be that as it may, I have now come to realize the truth of Walt Whitman's lines from "A Song of The Rolling Earth":

The gift is to the giver, and comes back most to him—it cannot fail.

MURRAY SEASONGOOD was born in Cincinnati on October 27, 1878, and has lived there throughout his life. He was educated at Harvard University, receiving his A.B. degree in 1900, his M.A. in 1901, and his LL.B. in 1903. Following his admission to the Ohio Bar in 1903, he began practicing law in Cincinnati. He has been a member of the Cincinnati Bar Association since 1904, and its president in 1945–6, as well as a long-time member of the American and Ohio Bar Associations and of the American Law Institute.

While his principal occupation has been as a lawyer, he has also found time for political, cultural, religious, educational, and philanthropic efforts. In 1923 he started an independent reform movement in Cincinnati, and became the first mayor elected (for two terms, 1926–30) under the city's amended charter. He also helped, beginning in 1926, to transform the local county government, and was president of the Hamilton County Good Government League from its founding in 1934 until 1945. From 1925 to 1959 he was part-time professor of law (now emeritus) at the University of Cincinnati; and in 1947–8, visiting professor at the Harvard Law School.

Mr. Seasongood has been, since 1902, almost continuously active in the Legal Aid movement, serving as president of the Legal Aid Society of Cincinnati (1930–6) and of the National Association of Legal Aid Societies (1945–8). One of his greatest devotions has been to the cause of improving local government, and he served as president of the National Municipal League (1931–4). He has written extensively for magazines and law journals, and his previous books include *Local Government in the United States: A Challenge and an Opportunity* (1933), and *Cases on the Law of Municipal Corporations* (1934, 1941, 1953). He married Agnes Senior of Cincinnati in 1912, and they have a daughter, Janet Hoffheimer, and three grandchildren.

July 1960

A NOTE ON THE TYPE

This book was set on the Linotype in ELECTRA, *designed by* W. A. *Dwiggins. The Electra face is a simple and readable type suitable for printing books by present-day processes. It is not based on any historical model, and hence does not echo any particular time or fashion. It is without eccentricities to catch the eye and interfere with reading—in general, its aim is to perform the function of a good book printing-type: to be read, and not seen.*

The book was composed, printed, and bound by Kingsport Press, Inc., Kingsport, Tennessee. Paper manufactured by P. H. Glatfelter Co., Spring Grove, Pennsylvania. Typography and binding design by Vincent Torre.